THE A TO Z OF
EVERYDAY THINGS

THE A TO Z OF EVERYDAY THINGS

JANICE WEAVER

Illustrations by Francis Blake

Tundra Books

Text copyright © 2004 by Janice Weaver
Illustrations copyright © 2004 by Francis Blake

Published in Canada by Tundra Books,
481 University Avenue, Toronto, Ontario M5G 2E9

Published in the United States by Tundra Books of Northern New York,
P.O. Box 1030, Plattsburgh, New York 12901

Library of Congress Control Number: 2004105082

National Library of Canada Cataloguing in Publication

Weaver, Janice
The A to Z of everyday things / Janice Weaver ; illustrator, Francis Blake.

Includes bibliographical references and index.
ISBN 0-88776-671-4

1. Handbooks, vade-mecums, etc. – Juvenile literature. 2. Curiosities and wonders –
Juvenile literature. I. Blake, Francis II. Title.

AG5.W39 2004   j031.02   C2004-902205-9

We acknowledge the financial support of the Government of Canada through the
Book Publishing Industry Development Program (BPIDP) and that of the
Government of Ontario through the Ontario Media Development Corporation's
Ontario Book Initiative. We further acknowledge the support of the Canada
Council for the Arts and the Ontario Arts Council for our publishing program.

Typeset in Bembo by M&S, Toronto

Printed and bound in Canada

1 2 3 4 5 6   09 08 07 06 05 04

For Mark, whose enthusiasm is always genuine,

even if his information is sometimes suspect

Acknowledgments

As always, I owe a great debt to my ever-expanding circle of first readers, especially my parents, Robert and Audrey Weaver (who naturally love everything I do, but also never hesitate to tell me when I could do it better); my good friends and sounding boards Caryl Silver, Terri Nimmo, and Sun-Kyung Yi; and the many people who offered up suggestions aplenty whenever I was stuck on a letter. The folks at Tundra Books – Kristy Button, Catherine Mitchell, Alison Morgan, Kong Njo, Melanie Storoschuk, Tamara Sztainbok, and Sue Tate – were as supportive and encouraging as ever. I must thank, especially, my long-time friend and publisher, Kathy Lowinger, for giving me the time to get this book right.

My editor, Gena Gorrell, does triple duty as friend and mentor. Not only did she give me my first job in publishing, but she has taught me almost everything I know about careful and diplomatic editing, skills she certainly had to call on in dealing with me on this project.

I could not have finished this book without the help of the Ontario Arts Council's Writers' Reserve Program and its publisher-recommenders, especially James Lorimer & Company and Maple Tree Press.

And what can I possibly say about Francis Blake? I couldn't have known, when I picked his artwork out of an agent's catalogue, that I was choosing not only a creative collaborator without equal but also a wonderful new friend. He is a huge talent and a tremendous pleasure to work with, and I'm grateful for everything he has brought to this book.

Contents

Introduction

A writer I really admire once said, "Common things . . . are the most important things, the ones with history and politics and meaning, the ones with clout." She's right. There is something truly amazing about the objects we routinely take for granted. They are the things we least question – or even think about – but they often tell us the most about ourselves and what we believe in. There is just something extraordinary in the ordinary.

I have filled this book with stories about twenty-six of those extraordinary ordinary things, one for each letter of the alphabet. Some are seemingly simple innovations, like the calendar or zero, that have had an immeasurable impact on the way we live our lives. Others, like forks and pretzels, are just everyday objects that nevertheless tell us something about who we are now or how we used to be.

For every one of the twenty-six letters, I hope, we learn something surprising and new – about the connection between Valentine's Day and wolves, for example, or how pretzels helped save a city from invasion. We learn why we fear the number thirteen and how Marco Polo brought ice cream to the Western world. We discover why widows wear black, why the Easter bunny hides eggs, why broken mirrors bring bad luck, and why yawning is contagious. We even find the stories of our efforts to measure time and to capture the sounds of our speech in symbols that people separated by centuries can still understand.

Ultimately, then, this is a book about ideas. Most everything in these pages had to be invented by the human mind, just as we invented cars and electrical power and the polio vaccine. But these things are now so much a part of our daily lives that we can barely imagine a time when they didn't exist – or, for that matter, conceive of the great struggle that often went into perfecting them or getting others to accept them. In fact, they have so successfully worked themselves into our everyday lives that it's hard not to take them for granted. In this book, I hope to shine some light on these remarkably unremarkable things, and, in doing so, paint a sometimes surprising picture of modern life and how we got here.

A

The Alphabet

I n the mid-1990s, two archeologists exploring a forgotten
Egyptian valley on the edge of the Sahara Desert found some
ancient inscriptions carved into the chalky face of a cliff. These
inscriptions – two lines of strange-looking symbols, including
human stick figures and wavy lines and crosses – were clearly not
hieroglyphics, the Egyptian picture writing. So what were they?
After several years of furious debate, the archeologists and their
colleagues concluded they were letters – more than that, they
were the oldest example of alphabetic writing ever found.

The discovery, just outside the city of Luxor, along the Nile
River, placed the invention of the alphabet about three hundred
years earlier (to 2000 B.C.) and in a different country (Egypt, not
Canaan) than was previously thought. It also raised a number of
questions. Who invented the alphabet? Why do our modern

letters look the way they do? Why do we have twenty-six of them, instead of twenty or thirty or a hundred? Why are so many languages written in letters representing sounds, when others use pictures or characters to represent whole words?

The alphabetic writing found at Luxor was Semitic, a language related to Hebrew and Arabic. Experts believe that the symbols were copies of about twenty-five simple Egyptian hieroglyphs (see sidebar), adapted to fit the Semitic language. They think that laborers from Semitic lands like Sinai and the Arabian peninsula came to Egypt – at the time, the wealthiest, most advanced empire in the world – to work and to serve in the Egyptian army. One of these foreign workers (or perhaps a whole team of foreigners working together) must have been familiar enough with those twenty-five hieroglyphs and the idea they represented – that the sounds of speech could be captured in written symbols – to think of creating something similar for his own language.

That first Semitic alphabet probably had twenty-seven letters, all of them consonants. (Although we must have vowels to be able to read and understand English – without them, what I just wrote would be an incomprehensible "lthgh w mst hv vwls t b bl t rd nd ndrstnd nglsh" – many ancient languages, and some modern ones, made do with consonants alone.) Taking their cue from the clever Egyptians, the inventors of the Semitic alphabet chose pictures to represent these twenty-seven letters. Their first letter, for example, was *aleph*, the Semitic word for "ox." The letter was drawn as a kind of stylized ox's head with two horns, which are today the two "feet" of the uppercase A. The thirteenth letter in their alphabet was *mem*, meaning "water." For that letter, they created a simplified version of the Egyptian hieroglyph for water – a squiggly line – and with a little imagination, we can still see that squiggly line in our own thirteenth letter, M.

Around 1000 B.C., the Semitic alphabet was picked up by a group of people known as the Phoenicians, who lived in what is

How Do You Spell That?

Egyptian hieroglyphics were quite complex and difficult to learn. There were about seven hundred different symbols in common use around 2000 B.C., roughly the time the Semitic alphabet was invented, and most were not easy to draw. In fact, because the hieroglyphic system was so complicated, only scribes and the elite members of society had the time and ability to master it. A simplified version, called hieratic, did spread to some middle-class landowners and army officers, but most other Egyptians, as well as the foreigners who came to the great empire to work, were unable to read and write.

The hieroglyphic system was called picture writing because it used little pictographic symbols to represent words and ideas. For example, the Egyptians had a symbol that looked something like a modern traffic light. That little picture was meant to represent a scribe's tools (it's actually a block of wood with paint bowls in it). But what made the hieroglyphic system so difficult to learn was that the same symbol could also mean the verb "to write." Figuring out how the symbol was being used could be a challenge.

There were, however, twenty-five hieroglyphs that represented single sounds, just as the letters of our alphabet do. A hieroglyph of an owl, for instance, meant not just the word "owl" but also the sound *m*. The inventor of the Semitic alphabet likely saw these twenty-five symbols and realized that they represented a way of expressing the sounds of spoken language in a style of writing so simple that even a child could learn it. And so was born the idea of the alphabet.

now Lebanon, and they fashioned it to fit their own language. The Phoenician alphabet had twenty-two letters, and nineteen of these can still be found, in modified form, in the English alphabet today. (The letters J, V, W, and X were added later, and two Phoenician letters gave rise to five letters in the modern alphabet.)

Like most great inventions, the alphabet was seized upon by any number of people and adapted to suit their needs. Greek traders, for example, saw what the Phoenicians were doing and, sometime around 800 B.C., borrowed their letters and created the Greek alphabet, the next branch of the family tree. Many of the letters of that alphabet are identical to our equivalent letters today, and the Greeks even gave us the word "alphabet," from *alpha* and *beta*, the first two letters in their system.

Next came the Romans, adopting the Greek alphabet for their own language, Latin. Because the Roman Empire stretched in its day from northern Africa to southern Europe and even as far as Britain, this was a key step in the alphabet's slow but steady progress around the world. Latin gave rise to new languages – including French, Italian, and Spanish – in all corners of the Roman Empire, and each of these new languages also made use of the empire's existing alphabet. This is why, to this day, the twenty-six letters we use to read and write English are actually known as the Roman alphabet.

The beauty of the modern Roman alphabet is its simplicity. Its twenty-six tiny letters can be put together in combinations to create any number of words in any number of languages. Today the Roman alphabet is the alphabet of choice for about two billion of the world's people, speaking more than a hundred different languages. It is so wonderfully uncomplicated that it's often possible for people to sound out words in a language they've never seen before, as long as that language also uses the Roman alphabet.

We can get a good sense of the genius of our system if we compare it to the beautiful but immensely complex Chinese script, which consists of a staggering 50,000 characters. In English, you need to learn only twenty-six letters to be able to form at least 600,000 – and perhaps many millions – of words. But in Chinese, you would need to memorize approximately 4,000 of the most commonly used characters just to be able to read your daily newspaper! Perhaps it's no surprise, then, that three-quarters of the people in the world use alphabetic scripts – including those who write Arabic (used in the Middle East and North Africa) and Cyrillic (used mostly in Russia).

The alphabet is perhaps the most important and longest-lasting invention of all time. Just try to imagine communicating something without it. If I wanted to get out the information in this book, for example, I would have to memorize every-thing that's here, then go to all my potential readers, one at a time or in small groups, and repeat it to them. In fact, this is precisely what the great ancient poets – Homer is the best-known example – did, singing or reciting their works over the course of many, many hours at festivals and other special events.

Lucky for Homer, the Greek alphabet was invented sometime during his lifetime, and the theory is that the blind poet eventually dictated his two famous epic poems, the *Odyssey* and the *Iliad*, and thus gave them a permanence that stories passed on orally can never achieve. There's no question that things that are written down pass more readily, and with fewer errors, from one generation to the next – that's why we still have the *Odyssey* and the *Iliad* when the oral poems that preceded them were lost. In fact, many scholars believe that the invention of the alphabet was directly responsible for the

Chinese is a pictographic (or logographic) writing system. In pictographic systems, pictures or characters are used to represent entire words, instead of syllables or single letters. Sometimes, two pictographs are combined to form one word. The Chinese word for "computer," for instance, is created by bringing together the symbols for "electric" and "brain."

great influence of Greek culture in general on Western society.

In a very real sense, the alphabet allows us to send thoughts from the mind of the writer to the mind of the reader, and that means that ideas can be more easily exchanged. We can pass them on without misrepresenting them or corrupting them with errors, so they become the building blocks of better, more sophisticated ideas down the road. In that sense, modern science, philosophy, literature, medicine – really any advanced idea you could name – owe their very existence to those twenty-six simple letters that changed the world.

Black

W e tend to link colors with emotions. We turn green with envy, are yellow with cowardice, and see red when we are angry. Orange, which conjures up images of sunshine and flames, suggests warmth and happiness, while blue, the color of water, is calming and constant.

For a long time, people thought of all colors simply as variations of black or white, and sometimes red. It wasn't until the 1700s that we began to learn about the relationship between light and color. Scientists realized that light is a type of energy that travels in waves of various lengths, and that light of different wavelengths appears to us as different colors. We now know that we are able to perceive a spectrum of light that ranges from violet (the shortest wavelength) to red (the longest). To remember the order of colors in the spectrum, or in a rainbow, we think of a man called Roy G. Biv – not a real person, of course, but an acronym for red, orange, yellow, green, blue, indigo, and violet.

We now say that black and white are not colors at all. White is what we see when all the colors of the spectrum come together, while black is the absence of light and hence color. But interestingly, we tend to think of things the other way around, with black the result of all the colors mixing into one and white the lack of color altogether.

Black is the most abused hue. Traditionally, it has been associated with evil, death, misfortune, and dark, depressing moods. We talk of blackmail, black markets, black magic, blackguards, and blacklisting. The bubonic plague's grim rampage through Europe was called the Black Death because it actually turned victims' skin black. People who are broken and bruised are said to be black and blue, not purple and yellow, which would be closer to the truth.

In Eastern cultures like China and Japan, where death is celebrated as a transition into a better life beyond the grave, white is the color of mourning instead of black.

In the West, black is also the color of mourning, although, according to legend, widows first started wearing it not as a symbol of woe but as a sort of disguise. The theory was that black clothes would make new widows less recognizable to the ghosts of their recently departed husbands, who, it was feared, might otherwise be tempted to rise from their freshly dug graves and haunt their former mates. Over time, the practice evolved, and black came to be seen as the perfect outward expression of inner grief. Queen Victoria is probably the modern world's most famous mourner; she donned black on the death of her husband, Prince Albert, in 1861, and was still wearing it when she died herself forty years later.

But many people feel that black has been unfairly tarnished. Viewed more positively, it is serious and solemn, discreet and not too showy. The Puritans – seventeenth-century religious reformers who wanted to simplify, or *purify*, the Christian church – recognized this, and they were perhaps the first people to deliberately adopt a predominantly black wardrobe. To them, black conveyed a message of self-discipline and sober hard work. The Puritans had no time to worry about how they looked, or to be led down the garden path by frivolous colors like yellows and reds.

Eventually, the Puritan movement died out, but those industrious people have nevertheless left their mark. This is especially true in the United States, where in 1628 the most successful early European colony – the Massachusetts Bay Colony – was established by a group of Puritans known as the Pilgrims. What we sometimes call a "puritanical attitude" lives on in North America in a general belief that our value as people is tied up in how hard we work and how much self-discipline we display.

Perhaps this is why there is such a fondness for black here. In big-city office towers from one coast to the other – towers that themselves are monochromatic monuments of glass, steel, and concrete – people shun bright colors in favor of "take me seriously" blacks, browns, and grays. No longer the harbinger of misfortune and doom, black now says sophistication and style – and it's slimming too!

C

Calendars

We humans are incurable clock-watchers. We like to mark time, kill time, save time, and play for time. Some of our most impressive intellectual achievements have come in our efforts to measure and organize time, from the invention of sundials and hourglasses to the advent of modern atomic clocks (which lose only about a second every million years and therefore are the most precise clocks ever made). We are the only species that divides our years into months, our months into weeks, our weeks into days, and our days into hours, minutes, and seconds.

Of all our struggles to understand time, the greatest centered around the quest to create a workable calendar. As much as thirteen thousand years ago, people began keeping track of the phases of the moon in an attempt to predict the changing of the seasons. Using the moon to measure time made sense to early people because, unlike the sun, the moon went through regular, easy-to-see phases as it waxed and waned. Those who were paying attention soon realized that these lunar phases repeated themselves about every twenty-nine days, and that if they counted the full moons between, say, the onset of winter and the coming of spring, they might be able to predict when these events would happen in the future.

We know that lunar calendars were used by many different groups of people, including the Babylonians, the early Greeks and Romans, and the Chinese. In fact, people in China still make use of their lunar calendar, which has since the 2600s B.C. been following twelve-year cycles, with each of the twelve years named for an animal. (The year 2004, for example, is 4701 and the year of the monkey.) All lunar calendars tend to be slightly different, but they usually consist of twelve months of twenty-nine or thirty days, for a lunar year of 354 days, which of course is eleven days short of the actual year.

This shortfall caused many centuries of chaos and confusion. Even in cultures with only a modest knowledge of astronomy, people soon realized that they were using the moon to try to predict what are actually solar (sun-related) events, like the changing seasons or the spring and fall equinoxes (see the entry on Easter). In an attempt to keep their lunar year in line with the solar year, some ancient people got quite creative. The Babylonians, for instance, alternated twelve years of twelve lunar months and seven years of thirteen lunar months, keeping them fairly closely on track with the solar cycle over a period of nineteen years. The early Greeks, by contrast, just inserted extra months at irregular intervals, greatly confusing everyone.

The ancient Egyptians were the first to think of using a calendar based on the sun instead of the moon. More than six thousand years ago, they came up with the idea of having yearly cycles of twelve thirty-day months, with an additional five days added at the end to celebrate the birthdays of five important Egyptian gods. Historians believe that the Egyptians made the leap from moon to sun by watching the flooding of the Nile, an event crucial to their survival and so predictable that some have called the river a giant clock stretched out over thousands of miles. The Egyptians knew that the flooding had nothing to do with the phases of the moon, but instead seemed to happen whenever the Dog Star, Sirius, lined up with the sun. In time, they also realized that this star showed up about a quarter of a day later with each passing year. Although they didn't know quite what to do about it, they concluded that the solar year was actually 365 ¼ days long.

Other people also came to use the sun to measure the passing of time – most notably, the Druids at Stonehenge, in southwestern England, and the Maya of Central America – but the Egyptian calendar was the one that eventually spread to the rest of the Western world. Julius Caesar learned of the Egyptians' sophisticated time-keeping methods while he was in Alexandria in 48 B.C., pursuing his mortal enemy, Pompey, and romancing Cleopatra, the alluring Egyptian queen. When he finally got around to returning to Rome, sometime the next year, he took the idea of the calendar – and an Egyptian astronomer – with him. The Roman Empire, he'd decided, would have had a solar calendar of its own.

The Romans had desperately needed a new calendar. Their haphazard approach to adding the days that would keep the lunar and solar years in line meant that, by Julius Caesar's time, their seasons were about three months out of whack. To fix this problem, Caesar's Egyptian astronomer recommended starting fresh with a calendar of twelve months of alternating lengths of thirty and thirty-one days. February would have twenty-nine days for three years in a row and thirty days every fourth year (called the leap year), taking care of that leftover quarter of a day the Egyptians had noticed.

Julius Caesar must have been an impatient man, for he decided it was best to change calendars as quickly as possible. To get the dates lined back up with the seasons, however, the year 46 B.C. stretched on for 445 days! People took to calling it the Year of Confusion – a reference not just to all those extra days but also to the monumental change Caesar was foisting upon his entire empire.

But Caesar was right, of course, and things ran much more smoothly after his reforms took effect on January 1, 45 B.C. His new system was so accurate, in fact, that the only significant change to the calendar between Caesar's time and 1582 A.D.

Naming the Months

The original Roman lunar calendar had only ten months, for a year of just 304 days. The months were called Martius, Aprilis, Maius, Junius, Quintilis, Sextilis, September, October, November, and December. The first four months were named for Roman gods, while the final six were from the words for five, six, seven, eight, nine, and ten.

Around 700 B.C., an ancient Roman king named Numa added two more months, Januarius and Februarius, to the end of the year, to bring it up to 355 days. When Julius Caesar reformed the calendar, however, he changed the date of the new year from March 25 to January 1, making the newest additions the first two months of the year, instead of the last. This is why September, October, November, and December – the months named for seven through ten – are now the ninth, ten, eleventh, and twelfth months.

came during the reign of his successor, Augustus Caesar. He started tinkering with the calendar to correct a minor inconsistency that had crept in when the Romans got confused and began having leap years every three years, instead of every four. Soon he had the brilliant idea of forcing his senators to name a month after him – they had earlier changed Quintilis to Julius (now July) to honor his predecessor, after all – and what had been Sextilis became Augustus, or what we now call August. It wouldn't do for Augustus's month, at thirty days, to be shorter than Caesar's, however, so the emperor "borrowed" a day from February and rearranged the months from September to the end of the year, ruining Caesar's clever practice of alternating months of thirty and thirty-one days.

The only other problem with the Roman calendar didn't reveal itself for hundreds and hundreds of years. Caesar and his Egyptian advisers had been slightly wrong in calculating the year at 365 days and 6 hours (or a quarter of a day). In fact, the solar year is 365 days, 5 hours, 48 minutes, and 45 seconds long. This minor miscalculation meant that the earth was gaining one extra day about every 130 years. By 1582, when the next major reform began, the calendar was ten days out of date.

The final calendrical reforms were the work of Pope Gregory XIII, who gave us our modern calendar, which we call the Gregorian calendar in his honor. He agreed to correct the Romans' miscalculation because various advisers convinced him that he – like all other Catholics – was celebrating the church's holy days ten days late. To get things back on track once again, he dropped ten days from October 1582. He then declared that although most years divisible by 4 would be leap years, those marking centuries would *not* be leap years unless they could be divided by 400. That is why the year 2000 was a leap year, while 1800 and 1900 were not. This prevents those pesky extra days from sneaking in again in the future.

Not everyone jumped right on the Gregorian calendar band-wagon, however. There's always great resistance whenever someone starts messing with time itself – especially when that someone is a religious leader, not a scientist or even an elected official – and many countries that were using the Julian calendar took hundreds of years to accept Pope Gregory's reforms. In Britain and her colonies, the Gregorian calendar was adopted only in 1752. By then, eleven days had to be dropped to bring everything back in line. People went to bed on September 2 that year and woke up the next morning on September 14, with many convinced that their lives had somehow been shortened by eleven days. Others took it all in stride, with one man jokingly complaining to the newspaper that though he seemed to have been dozing for more than a week, he felt he wasn't "any more refreshed than after a common night's sleep."

Even in our own day, the issue of calendar reform is alive and well. Some people would like to see a more logical calendar, with every year and every month starting on the same day of the week (this could be achieved by organizing the year into thirteen months of four weeks each). Others are bothered that our months vary in length and would like to return to the truly ancient system of having twelve months of thirty days, with five special days added at the end of the year. One real problem is that the Gregorian calendar runs fast by about twenty-six seconds, a situation made worse by the fact that the earth's rotation has been slowing ever so slightly over the years. Scientists speculate that sometime around 4900, our calendar will be off by an entire day, and no doubt the whole process of reform will have to begin all over again.

D

Diamonds

In 1867, the young son of a South African farmer brought a shiny pebble back from a nearby river to use in a game. The farmer, who had an inkling that this was no ordinary stone, picked it up and drew it down one of the farmhouse windows. When it scratched the glass, he knew exactly what he had: a diamond in the rough.

To the untrained eye, rough diamonds are hard to spot. In fact, people living around that South African farm, in a region then called the Transvaal, had probably been finding and tossing away rough diamonds for years. When miners and fortune-seekers heard of the farmer's discovery and began making their way to the area by the thousands, they reportedly found diamonds sticking out of the mud walls of some of the local homes. For three decades, the Transvaal's Dutch-born farmers had been trying to scratch out a humble living from the rocky landscape, and that whole time they had been sitting on a diamond field worth billions of dollars.

Diamonds are made of layers of carbon that get pressed together, forming a crystal. They are among the most ancient objects in the universe. Scientists have recovered from meteorites microscopic diamonds – called nanodiamonds – that are older than our solar system. Using a space telescope, they have also found diamonds dancing in the dust of stars, proof that they still float out in space to this day. They also exist way beneath the surface of this planet, stuck in rock about a hundred miles (160 kilometers) down.

Earthly diamonds were first discovered thousands of years ago in the sand of riverbeds, and until very recently, that is where all diamonds came from. People didn't mine for the stones, but instead simply dug them out or picked them up from the banks and bottoms of streams and other bodies of water. In the late 1800s, however, diamond hunters began to think that perhaps these small clusters of gems had come from somewhere else. Soon someone suggested that most of the world's diamonds had probably been carried from deep within the earth by now extinct volcanoes called pipes, and that these pipes, if they could be found, could be an incredibly rich source of gems.

The search for diamond-bearing pipes stretched out over the next hundred years. Today it is believed that all of the world's roughly six thousand pipes have been identified, though only a handful of those contain enough diamonds to be worth mining. In parts of the world, the hunt for those few rich pipes seemed to be lifted right from the pages of a spy novel. In northern Canada, where a group of valuable pipes was found in the mid-1990s, workers would go out to collect soil samples wearing camouflage gear to hide themselves and their activities from planes passing overhead. Sometimes, geologists have been sent to gather rock samples without even being told what they were supposed to be looking for.

This aura of secrecy is typical of the diamond business, and it's one of the reasons the gems are prized so much more than other stones. There's a mystique, a mystery to diamonds that other jewels just don't have. Part of that comes from centuries of diamond lore, stories about legendary gems that have cursed or blessed their owners. The rest is created by the giant diamond companies, which control the world's supply of stones and work hard to convince consumers that diamonds are the ultimate proof of their wealth and sophistication.

Advertising has played a huge role in persuading people that though they serve no real purpose, diamonds are something they simply must have. A 1940s De Beers ad gave us the line "A diamond is forever" – called the greatest ad slogan of the twentieth century – and ever since then, diamond rings have been inextricably linked with love, marriage, and eternity. In 2004, some clever dealers began promoting the idea of a right-hand ring that women would buy for themselves as a symbol of their independence and success. Pushed with the slogan "Your left hand says 'we.' Your right hand says 'me,'" these rings are aimed at single or divorced women with a lot of money to spare – smart marketing in an age when marriage rates are falling and divorce rates climbing.

Today, diamond companies around the world face a real threat from so-called blood diamonds, gems that have been used to finance a monstrous, decades-long civil war in Sierra Leone, in Africa. Consumers want proof that the stones they buy have not been tainted – proof that's almost impossible to provide, since it's very difficult to tell where a particular stone was dug out of the ground. Still, the great diamond mines in the north of Canada are now using lasers to etch a picture of a polar bear on each

Hope Springs Eternal

The world's most famous stone is probably the Hope Diamond, which isn't the largest one ever found but does have the most colorful history. It began life as the French Blue in the hands of Louis XIV in the 1660s, then was stolen during the French Revolution by a professional thief who had been set free from jail by a rioting mob of Parisians. For two hundred years, no one knew what had become of the French Blue, though the theory now is that to disguise its identity, the thieves quickly had the stone recut into the much smaller but no less beautiful dark blue diamond we know as the Hope.

The Hope Diamond has never been able to shake its associations with bad luck and misfortune. There are stories (mostly false) that it was originally stolen from the eye of a Hindu statue in India, and that its many owners have been, variously, torn apart by wild dogs, shot in fits of jealous rage, and beheaded by the guillotine. Even the Hopes, the wealthy banking family who bought the stone in 1830, ended up in bankruptcy court, hawking the diamond to the highest bidder.

Today the Hope Diamond sits encased in bullet-proof glass in a hall of the Smithsonian Institution in Washington, D.C. Its notorious history has proved very good for business: every year, it draws more visitors than any other item in the museum's entire collection.

gem, and De Beers has developed a secret process for inscrib-ing its products with a logo and serial number that are invisible to the naked eye. Everyone involved with the industry agrees that the trade in blood diamonds must be stopped before it sparks a worldwide boycott of all stones, the greatest menace diamonds have faced since they first danced through space so many billions of years ago.

E

Easter

According to an ancient tale from India, there once was a band of four wandering animals – a water bird, a monkey, a fox, and a hare. These four had vowed to live in harmony with nature, never killing another living thing. To test their commitment, a god disguised himself as a beggar and pleaded with them for food. The first three all brought him things that had been abandoned by others, which did honor their pledge not to kill but also required no sacrifice of their own. When it was the hare's turn, he nobly volunteered to cook *himself* to satisfy the poor man's hunger. The god was so moved that he revealed his true identity and declared the humble bunny the most virtuous creature in the land. He then carved the figure of the hare onto the face of the moon, so everyone in the world would be able to see him and remember his selfless offer.

This rather gruesome tale of personal sacrifice and the symbolism of the moon gets repeated, in slightly different forms, in countries around the world. In the West, we can find elements of the story in what is perhaps the most important holiday in the Christian year, Easter, bound up as it is with the sacrifice of Christ, Easter bunnies, and the coming of the full moon.

There are hints that the Easter festival actually existed before the Bible. The word Easter likely comes from Eostre, the name of an ancient pagan (pre-Christian) goddess of spring. Some say the holiday really celebrates not Christ's rebirth but the rebirth of all life after the dark, cold "death" of winter. Indeed, Easter is overflowing with symbols of new life, from eggs and rabbits (which, because they have so many young, represent fertility) to the moon (which wanes and waxes, or dies and is reborn, every month).

Easter is always on a Sunday, but it can fall anywhere between March 22 and April 25. In 325 A.D., church fathers began determining the date using a formula that said the holiday had to be celebrated on the Sunday that follows the first full moon after the spring equinox. (Christians believe that Jesus was crucified under a full moon.) Ironically, this formula was impossible for people of the fourth century to implement, since, unlike us, they had no way of accurately predicting the movements of the moon and the sun. But the link between Easter and the cycles of nature is a holdover from the days when people believed in multiple gods and looked to the moon and the sun and phenomena like eclipses and comets to predict future events. Today, almost every other important moment in the Christian calendar is observed on the same day year after year, but Easter is still at the mercy of the movements of the moon.

Like the moon, the spring equinox was critical to the Easter calculations because it also symbolizes rebirth and new beginnings. We even used to celebrate the new year on March 25, a date that was chosen because it was near the equinox. The less logical date

Just What Is an Equinox?

We have two equinoxes each year, one in March and one in September. These are the days when the sun is directly above the equator. They are also the only two times a year when the days and nights are of roughly equal length (twelve hours apiece) every-where around the world.

The spring equinox, also called the vernal equinox, occurs sometime between March 19 and 21. The autumnal equinox is always on September 22 or 23. In the northern hemisphere, these two days mark the coming of spring and the coming of fall. Traditionally, the two equinoxes have been important feast days in many different religions.

of January 1 became the start of the new year when the Gregorian calendar was adopted. (For more, see the entry on calendars.)

All of this emphasis on rebirth and new beginnings explains why, although rabbits give birth to live young, the Easter rabbit – a *male* rabbit, no less – comes bearing eggs, another symbol of life. Some observers have taken the imagery even further, claiming that the round, white eggshell represents the moon and the yellow yolk the sun.

Eggs were once considered a special treat because people were prohibited from eating them for the forty days leading up to Easter, a period called Lent. Nowadays, to keep the thrill of the egg alive, we have to make it out of chocolate. The modern Easter bunny hides his eggs on Saturday night for children to find on Sunday morning. Unlike Santa, who favors those who've been nice over those who've been naughty, the Easter bunny makes no moral judgments. The quickest kids – and maybe the sneakiest, or at least the ones who know the best hiding places – reap the greatest Easter rewards.

Sometimes people still engage in the rather odd practice of rolling eggs against one another or down a hill. This tradition supposedly symbolizes the rock that was miraculously rolled away from the mouth of Jesus' tomb at the time of his resurrection. The most famous egg-rolling party takes place on the White House lawn, with as many as ten thousand children gathering to play games, hear stories, and decorate their own Easter eggs.

In other parts of the world, historians have unearthed several Easter traditions that were perhaps even stranger than our own. At one time, in what is now the Czech Republic, boys would celebrate the holiday by striking girls with willow branches until they handed over eggs they had decorated. In England, men would lift women into the air and carry them as far as they could, with the women returning the favor the following day. And in Germany, Easter eggs were hidden in thorny, prickly bushes so children would get scratched and stung as they retrieved them.

Today Easter, like Christmas, is for many people an entirely secular (non-religious) holiday, and certainly most of us don't recognize any connection between it and the cycles of the moon. Like Santa Claus at Christmas, the Easter bunny provides a way for all of us to enjoy this celebration of spring, even if we don't happen to share the religious beliefs that are attached to it too.

F

Forks

For hundreds of years, writers of all stripes have been offering up advice on etiquette, good manners, and the importance of following the customs of the times. Some of the advice given in centuries past seems bizarre and even shocking to us today. Most of us do not need to be told, as people of the 1500s were, that it isn't polite to blow your nose into the tablecloth, or that if you are overcome by a sudden need to vomit, you should leave the room first. To people of the sixteenth century, however, these could be murky waters indeed.

The key to proper etiquette – in any society, at any time in history – is to learn which behaviors are considered acceptable and which are not. But because times and societies change, our notions of proper conduct do too. In the 1930s, a sociologist named Norbert Elias began studying books on Western manners from about the 1500s on. He wanted to chart the evolution of so-called civilized behavior over four centuries, and to use that as a basis for a theory about Western society in general. The books Elias studied offered advice on facial expressions, modes of dress, and conduct in church, but they zeroed in most often on what we now call table manners.

Some of our most complex cultural rituals, Elias quickly concluded, surround sharing meals with others. Almost as soon as we are old enough to begin feeding ourselves, we learn that there is a seemingly endless supply of rules that our mothers really would like us to follow. We shouldn't talk with our mouths full, we're told, or eat with our elbows on the table. And we should never take food directly from a knife (the potential for stabbing ourselves is too great, perhaps, and nothing ruins a nice dinner party quite like the need for an ambulance), instead always transfering small portions to a fork first.

Things weren't always so complicated. Before the mid-1500s, people ate in a much more communal way than we do today. Paintings show diners sharing the same rough wooden boards (before someone thought of plates), and even drinking from the same glasses. They help themselves from large common dishes at the center of the table or on sideboards, reaching in to pull out chunks of meat by hand. They also eat their various dishes in whatever order they please – no appetizers, main courses, and desserts for these people – lifting bowls right to their mouths to slurp back sauces and soups with delight.

This all started to change around 1570, when King Henri III brought the fork to France, probably after seeing it in use in Venice. It wasn't an instant hit. Many French people thought Henri, who was an unpopular ruler to begin with, was simply being pretentious. And he probably didn't help his own cause too much, since we're told that he and his courtiers were far from adept with the fork, which in those days had only two widely spaced tines, making it difficult to handle with poise. In Henri's case, more food apparently fell into his lap than made it to his mouth.

Henri had started a trend, however, and it proved to be unstoppable. Slowly at first, and then with increasing momentum, the fork caught on. To use one became the sign of a well-bred diner. And for those who were puzzled about exactly how this new instrument worked, there were soon numerous user's guides to help lift the fog of confusion. Don't lick your fork when it's dirty

Chopsticks and Rice

Since about the fourth century B.C., people in China have been eating their food with chopsticks. These graceful utensils, which later spread to many other Asian countries, were likely invented specifically to be used with rice. Indeed, they are ideal for all kinds of Asian dishes, which tend to consist of bite-size pieces of meat or seafood. This style of cooking made great logical sense in countries where the large, wet paddies used for rice production severely limited the amount of wood available for cooking. In the days before electricity, people depended on food that could be stir-fried quickly to save on fuel.

The shape of chopsticks mimics the thumb and forefinger, which is how people would once have taken their food, and their name is probably an English mangling of the Chinese *kuaizi*, meaning "nimble ones." In Japanese, the word for chopsticks is *hashi*, meaning "bridge," because they span the chasm from bowl to mouth.

or wipe it on the tablecloth, the uninitiated were advised, and try to avoid holding it in your fist like a stick or using it to transport liquids to your mouth. Though this seems obvious to us today, perhaps, if you'd never seen or used a fork before, these were the kinds of things you needed to know.

But why do we need forks at all? The commonly held belief is that eating with the hands is unsanitary, and therefore that the fork represents a more civilized, refined way to take food. Even in Henri's day, fork advocates began to suggest that "all men's fingers are not alike cleane." And while this was certainly some-thing to consider back when we were all dipping our possibly unwashed hands into communal bowls, is it really an issue today, when we eat from separate plates and no one else (except the cook) comes anywhere near to touching our food?

Over the years, people have offered other explanations for the rise of the fork. Norbert Elias argued that its arrival, which coincided with the appearance of individual plates and place settings, actually marked a shift in how we viewed other people. It was, he said, as if there rose up "an invisible wall . . . between one human body and another, repelling and separating." In fact, the place setting marks off our personal space at the dinner table, creating a physical boundary that we don't want our fellow diners to cross. In our clean, sanitized modern world, it seems, we have gone from sharing a meal to simply sharing a table.

Games

S oldiers fighting in the Trojan War – the conflict that inspired many of the greatest works of classical literature, as well as the movie with Brad Pitt – had a passion for a backgammon-like game known as *tablé*, often settling down for a spirited match even during breaks in the fighting. The Roman emperor Claudius was also obsessed with *tablé* (or its Roman equivalent, *tabula*), so much so that he reportedly had a board fitted into his carriage so he could play whenever he was on the road, overseeing his massive empire.

Claudius and the Trojan warriors were not alone, for game playing is as old as human history. In ancient times, men tossed the heel bones of sheep, the forerunners to our modern dice, to determine whether they would be enslaved or set free. In the Bible, soldiers drew lots to decide who would get Jesus' robes after his crucifixion. Rudimentary gaming boards have been unearthed at the tombs of the pharaohs, in the pews of medieval English churches, and even from underneath the ashes of the city of Pompeii, buried by a volcanic eruption almost two thousand years ago.

Most games – even those we still play today – have their origins in what are called divination rituals. These ceremonies, common to virtually all ancient societies, were relied on to reveal the will of the gods. In their earliest form, small sticks or bits of animal bone would be tossed or drawn by a priest or a shaman, who would then read the future in the way the pieces fell or the order in which they were chosen. This information was used to advise people on everything from when to plant or harvest their crops to when to go to war.

Later divination rituals made use of dice and strips of oiled paper. The ancient Greeks, for example, cast dice to consult Zeus and other gods, and Greek soldiers sometimes did the same to determine the order the gods wanted them to follow into battle. The strips of oiled paper, which were first used in Korea and traveled from there to China (where they were called stick cards, and were part of a drinking game) and on to the rest of the world, evolved in Europe into tarot cards, still used now for fortune-telling.

Over time, people stopped seeing the world as a place ruled by powers beyond human control, and they felt less need to consult gods and goddesses for clues on how to live their lives. Dice and cards lost their fortune-telling properties and began to be used mostly for fun. On their own or with decorated boards and other game pieces, they became a universal way to pass the time.

What's interesting is that many games that spring up independently in diverse and unconnected societies show surprising similarities. Versions of the game of jacks, for instance, were played in ancient Greece (with the knucklebones of sheep), in

The I Ching

Perhaps as early as 1100 B.C., Chinese diviners were tossing reeds or other small sticks and looking up the results in a book called the *I Ching*. This ancient text had sixty-four complicated, six-line diagrams that, it was thought, could predict the future. To consult the text, believers would toss their reeds, find the diagram that corresponded most closely to the pattern in which they landed, and then read the written interpretation that accompanied the diagram. Each one of the six lines in the diagram had a special meaning that could be used to guide conduct.

By the 500s B.C., the *I Ching* was being viewed more as a work of philosophy than as a fortune-telling tool. Confucius, the most distinguished philosopher in Chinese history, made the book famous, using it to promote the need for morality and personal responsibility among his followers.

Africa, and in the islands of the South Pacific. Cat's cradle, a childhood game that requires only a loop of string and a set of nimble fingers, can be found in communities from the Canadian Arctic to Australia.

Other games have simply evolved from their ancient counterparts and spread slowly around the world. Chess, for instance, was invented in India more than 1,300 years ago. Called *chaturanga*, the Indian game was designed to teach players about war strategy. The pieces were a king and his counselor, elephants, horses, chariots, and foot soldiers, the main elements of the Indian army at that time. (When the game spread to the West, these pieces were eventually transformed into the king and queen, bishops, knights, castles, and pawns.) An ancient Japanese strategy game, called *go*, was played by samurai warriors hoping to sharpen their tactical skills, and it was even taught as a course in the country's military academy.

Not all games were entirely divorced from their spiritual or religious roots, of course. In pachisi, often called the national game of India, the goal is for players to reach the kingdom of heaven. Hopscotch, which was originally taught to children by Roman soldiers as they built the cobbled roads (and ready-made hopscotch boards) connecting the various parts of their empire, came to represent the soul's journey from earth to heaven. (Some people believe hopscotch also recalls ancient myths of labyrinths and mazes, like the one that held the legendary Minotaur.) Even bowling was once a religious rite. Worshippers would roll a ball down a church cloister hoping to knock down pins that represented people who had strayed from the straight and narrow.

Today, thanks to computers and XBoxes and CD-ROMs, the world of gaming has been completely transformed. Now you can steer a high-performance car around a speedway, pilot a helicopter into combat, or box for the world heavyweight title. You can even immerse yourself in virtual worlds, strapping on a cyberglove and trying your luck against players from around the corner or across the globe. What would those Trojan warriors think?

H

Holidays

I n the late 1700s and early 1800s, the lives of people in many
parts of the world were turned upside down by the arrival of
power-driven machines and large factories, a period of history
we call the Industrial Revolution. In Europe and, to a lesser
extent, North America, the net of small-scale, rural communities was converted into a society of vast, densely populated cities.
The Industrial Revolution ushered in the era of mass production,
which made goods more affordable and improved the living stan-
dards of many, but not all. And it transformed both the kind of
work people did and the way they did it.

With industrialization, those who had once toiled outside at
physical work like farming found themselves in textile mills and
iron forges, slaving long hours at tedious, repetitive tasks. And
while work had previously been seasonal – with people laboring

feverishly through the spring, summer, and fall, then not at all through the winter – it was now year-round, often six and even seven days a week. Many workers put in seventy hours a week or more, and for their efforts they got perhaps two days' holiday a year (plus Sundays, if they were among the lucky ones).

The word "holiday" comes from "holy days," and in the pre-industrial era, these were the traditional periods of rest from work. They were religious feasts and festivals, celebrations honoring gods, saints, spirits, and even significant times of year, like the harvest or the summer and winter solstices. Then, as now, many Christian holy days recalled events in the life of Jesus, like his birthday (Christmas) and his resurrection (Easter). Jewish holy days mostly commemorated major events in Jewish history, including the Exodus from Egypt (Passover) and the second-century B.C. defeat of the Syrians (Hanukkah). Buddhist holy days marked key moments in the life of Buddha, such as his birth, his enlightenment, and his death. Other religions also celebrated important dates in their history and in the lives of their leaders.

For centuries, everyone observed holy days together, with religious services, special meals, and often parades or the exchanging of gifts. This was fine in the days when most people farmed modest parcels of land clustered around villages or worked in local shops as bakers or shoemakers. But with the advent of factories, and the much larger workforces needed to run them, it became a problem for all the laborers to have the same days off. Slowly, the number of holy days celebrated began to dwindle, and in the 1790s employers came up with the idea of staggering their workers' rest days, or what began to be called holidays, and asking them to take them in a block.

This idea must not have been too popular, for more than a century passed before it caught on. Many employees preferred to keep working, if only because their bosses had no intention of paying them while they were on holiday. It would be another three or four decades before the concept of paid vacations took hold.

The rise of the paid vacation coincided with a new fashion for suntanning. People had at one time frowned on tanned skin as a sign that you worked out-doors, and therefore were lower class. But like small-scale farming and quaint village life, that idea was also swept away by the Industrial Revolution. With factory workers stuck indoors all day, tanned skin became the new hallmark of upper-class life, proof that you were wealthy enough to spend your days at the beach instead of on the factory floor.

The Nazis of 1930s Germany were among the first to embrace the notion of paying workers while they were on holiday.

Soon, an entire industry – what we now call the tourism or leisure industry – was being built around getting people to those beaches to work on their tans or finding them other things to do to occupy their free time. While holy days had been full of reli-gious purpose, vacations were, by definition, empty periods of time ("vacation," like "vacant," comes from the Latin word *vacare*, meaning "to be empty"). Just as we once had to be forced to take block holidays at all, we now had to be encouraged to use our vacations to get away, to travel, to spend money. These days, many of us pass our working lives looking forward to those two or three weeks we get off – when we can finally blow all that money we devote the other fifty weeks to earning.

Ice Cream

When the explorer and trader Marco Polo returned to Italy from his travels in China in 1295, he brought back tales of a rich, technologically advanced society of bustling cities and towns. He wrote a book describing, among other things, fireworks, paper money, "large black stones that . . . burn away like charcoal" (which we now know was coal), and a postal system that saw riders on horseback carrying mail to the most distant corners of the country. (He neglected to mention several other things that any thirteenth-century visitor to China should have noticed, however, like foot-binding and the Great Wall, which has led some historians to claim that he never actually made it all the way there.)

Polo's report so astonished his fellow Venetians that they wouldn't believe most of what he told them. In fact, many people took to calling him "the man of a million lies." We know today that he did get quite a few things wrong. But much of his information — whether he gathered it first-hand or just repeated what he'd heard from other traveling merchants — was correct. The descriptions he provided eventually helped Europeans make for themselves many of the most wondrous Chinese inventions, including paper, movable type (see the entry on Xeroxing), and — thank heavens! — ice cream.

The Chinese version of ice cream was probably sweetened rice mixed with milk and then surrounded with ice and salt until it froze. (Ice and salt work together to produce a chemical reaction that draws heat away from other ingredients, causing them to freeze.) Italians took things a step further, using ice and salt to freeze cream, fruit, and spices. They brought these special desserts, called *gelati*, to the French court, probably in the late 1500s, and the *gelati* spread from there to the rest of Europe.

Initially, ice cream was a dessert exclusively for the rich. It was complicated and time-consuming to make, and therefore not intended for riff-raff. Also, since mechanical refrigeration didn't come into wide use until the mid-1800s, ice was pretty hard to come by. Stone wells and cellars, icehouses, and pits dug into the ground or the side of a hill provided a way to store the ice and snow that Mother Nature created in the winter. But in the hotter regions of southern Europe, where cool desserts were most in demand, it was difficult to find enough cold stuff to use in making the frosty treat. In the rare southern winters when the mercury really dropped, people would harvest ice and snow from frozen ponds and rivers, then pack it all away until it was needed to beat the summer heat. Many of the more northerly countries saw a great money-making opportunity in exporting something they certainly had a surplus of. Norway, for example, did a booming business selling ice to most of the rest of Europe in the 1800s — once some industrious merchant had figured out how to insulate his ships' holds at least enough to keep the cargo from melting before it reached its destination.

Ice cream came to America in the 1740s. There, the colder northern states could harvest winter ice and sell it to a ready-made market farther south. And with the introduction, in 1846, of the first machine for making ice cream – and then refrigerators, ice-cream parlors, and street vendors on bicycles – this one-time luxury found its way into the hearts and stomachs of ordinary people.

Today Americans remain the world's most faithful consumers of ice cream. U.S. factories make and sell enough each year for every man, woman, and child in the country to have a scoop a day – *every* day – for six months straight! For the most part, American ice-cream lovers are traditionalists; that old standby, vanilla, has cornered a whopping 29 percent of the market, with chocolate and strawberry following close behind. But in other parts of the world, bizarre flavors reign supreme. In Japan, for instance, the 2002 Ice Cream Exhibition spotlighted several varieties that are surely acquired tastes, including octopus, fried eggplant, ox tongue, and wasabi (horseradish paste). And in a small snack bar in the mountains of Venezuela, patrons can sample any one of more than seven hundred different flavors, from garlic and fried pork rind to champagne and tuna fish, a menu so diverse it earned the shopkeeper a spot in the *Guinness Book of World Records*.

In the 1920s, people arriving at Ellis Island, the American immigration station, were given ice cream – a treat so unfamiliar to them that many used their knives to spread it onto bread.

Jack-o'-lanterns

R ound and orange and often covered in warts, pumpkins
must have astonished the first American settlers when
they arrived in the New World in the 1620s. Apart from the few
descriptions that had made their way back to the Old World
aboard the ships of explorers from Christopher Columbus on
down, Europeans knew almost nothing of pumpkins, which are
native to North America. Certainly these remarkable vegetables –
or, some say, fruits – which can grow to be many hundreds of
pounds, made a lasting impact when they arrived in England and
France in the late 1600s. Charles Perrault, the French author of
Tales of Mother Goose, was impressed enough by the sight of a
pumpkin to have the fairy godmother transform one into
Cinderella's lavish coach. And in a popular nursery rhyme, Peter
is a pumpkin eater who puts his wife in a hollowed-out pumpkin

Trick or Treat!

Each year on November 1, the Celts, people who lived in Britain before Roman times, ushered in their new year. To them, the arrival of November marked the end of summer, the season of growth and life, and the start of the cold, dark, deathly winter. On the eve of their new year, October 31, they held a harvest festival called Samhain (literally "summer's end"), which was named for the Celtic lord of death, Saman. That night, children would go door to door, asking not for candy but for wood for a bonfire. All the villagers would then gather around this fire, sacrificing animals and examining their remains for signs of what the coming year would bring. Later that evening, they believed, those who'd died in the previous year would rise from their graves and roam the earth until dawn.

By the 600s, most Celts had converted to Christianity, though some of their ancient festivals lingered on. To provide a more appropriate, church-approved celebration to replace the Celts' festival of the dead, Pope Boniface IV named November 1 All Saints' Day, a time to honor the thousands of saints who didn't have their own special feast days. All Saints' Day was also known as All Hallows' Day ("hallow" is simply an old English word for a holy person), and the night before came to be called All Hallows' Eve, or, eventually, Halloween.

shell when he finds he can't control her behavior ("And there he kept her very well").

Perrault and the unknown author of "Peter, Peter, Pumpkin Eater" clearly understood that when they had been cleaned of their pulpy insides, pumpkins made excellent containers for everything from pretend princesses to wayward wives. In the New World, people also used them as lanterns, setting candles inside their stringy walls and puncturing them with holes to let out the light.

But the tradition of carving pumpkins for Halloween, surprisingly, did not originate in the pumpkin patches of the Thirteen Colonies. Instead, it migrated to America from Scotland and Ireland, where people have been making jack-o'-lanterns for centuries. The practice supposedly grew out of an Irish legend about a man called Stingy Jack. According to the story, Jack was a notorious miser who also had a mischievous streak. He tricked the Devil into climbing a tree, then carved the sign of a cross into its trunk so the demon could not climb down again. Trapped, the hapless Devil bought his freedom by agreeing not to claim Jack's soul when he died, which, as luck would have it, was just a short time later.

Spurned by God for his miserly ways and by the Devil for his constant pranks, Jack could not go to heaven *or* hell. Instead, he was sent to wander the earth for the rest of time, with only a burning coal to light his way. He put the glowing ember into a hollowed-out turnip, earning himself the nickname Jack of the Lantern, which he probably considered an improvement on Stingy Jack. Soon, people in Ireland and Scotland were making their own "jack-o'-lanterns" by carving spooky, scary faces into turnips and potatoes. They would set these unearthly creations in their windows to ward off Stingy Jack and all his ghostly comrades.

When immigrants from Ireland and Scotland made their way to America, they quickly discarded the lowly turnip in favor of the pumpkin. Big and round, the pumpkin reminded them of a human head – it's what the headless horseman hurls at Ichabod Crane in "The Legend of Sleepy Hollow" – so it was the ideal choice for the grotesque masks that were meant to scare away the spirits who roamed about on Halloween. As an added precaution, those who had to venture out on this frightful night would wear disguises so that any ghosts they happened to encounter would mistake them for their own ghoulish friends. Today, we keep this rather grim tradition alive in the pint-sized witches and goblins who haunt streets all over North America every October 31.

Kissing

There are a lot of geographic assumptions made about kissing. Most people the world over, for example, concede that the French are probably the best kissers. Deep, passionate smooching is called French kissing in English and many other languages, and the French are generally believed – true or not – to be more romantic and easier with displays of affection. The English, by contrast, are thought to be cold and emotionless, while North Americans supposedly hold too tightly to their Puritan past to be able to kiss freely – at least in public.

Many of these national preconceptions have been reinforced by differences in the practice of social kissing – that is, using kisses to greet family, friends, and even workmates. Anthropologists call social kissing an "access ritual." Like shaking hands and hugging, it is a sign that the greeter is opening herself up –

giving greater physical and emotional access – to the person she's greeting.

The social kiss has become more widespread in recent years, but it has been around for a long, long time. People often assume that it originated in rural France and progressed from there to the more cosmopolitan Paris and on to the rest of Europe. But the truth is that the normally reserved English were the masterminds of the social kiss. Writings from the fifteenth and sixteenth centuries tell of kisses flying fast and furious all over the sceptered isle. Even total strangers, it seems, would greet each other with a smack on the lips.

In fact, it was the French who cooled the English passion for kissing. By the late 1600s, French habits and customs had taken over the court of England, and the seventeenth-century Frenchman was a much less demonstrative creature than his modern counterpart. He liked refined, modest behavior, and especially preferred a low, formal bow to a kiss. Under the French influence, the English social kiss was quickly extinguished.

Kiss and Tell

We don't really know where the impulse to kiss comes from. Some scientists have suggested that it recalls the days before baby formula, when mothers would chew up food for their youngsters and pass the resulting mush from mouth to mouth through a gesture much like a kiss. It seems certain that kissing is not a learned behavior; most primates, like gorillas and chimpanzees, kiss to give comfort and show affection, which suggests it's a habit we don't need to be taught.

Today, social kissing is enjoying a resurgence in most of the Western world, particularly Europe. In North America, sadly, we tend to be much less comfortable with it, and we never quite seem to know the rules. Is it one cheek or two – or even three? Do you actually touch the cheek, or do you just kiss somewhere in its general vicinity? And how do you know when a kiss is an acceptable substitute for the more modest, less intimate handshake?

Women are generally more comfortable with social kissing than men are. They tend to know when to kiss and when not to, and they are equal-opportunity kissers, bussing both men and other women with quiet confidence. Men, on the other hand, reserve the social kiss for women only – at least in North America – and this has led to some confusion in the workplace. Is the social kiss, many men wonder, acceptable professional behavior if you are restricting it to only half your colleagues? Or does that amount to a form of gender discrimination?

Nowadays, the social kiss is usually a quick peck on or near one or both cheeks. Historically, however, the location of the kiss has depended on the social relationship between the greeters. Two people of equal standing would kiss on the mouth or cheek, but those on unequal footing would never dream of displaying such familiarity. People who ranked above you on the social ladder were rewarded with a kiss on the hand or on a ring, while those higher still got a kiss on the knee. And if you really wanted to demonstrate your inferiority, you kissed the hem of a person's garments, or even his feet. Social anthropologists have pointed out that this posture leaves your back wholly unprotected, and so is a symbol of your vulnerable relationship to the kissee: your crouching figure is ripe for a slap on the head or, worse yet, a dagger in the back.

Anthropologists estimate that about 90 percent of humans engage in kissing of a social or a romantic nature. The remaining

10 percent have found other ways to greet one another and show affection, including rubbing noses and cheeks. And while kissing has, at various points in history, been severely restricted – in Naples, Italy, in 1562, it was even made a crime punishable by death – we aren't so easily put off. Most of us would like to kiss more often, rather than less, and these days the benefits of kissing are rarely in dispute. Indeed, studies have shown that infants who are kissed and cuddled from their very first moments get a head start in life that is almost impossible for the kiss-deprived to overcome.

Even an unborn baby is capable of pursing its lips as if preparing for a kiss.

L

Lipstick

N o discussion of kissing would be complete if we didn't spend some time on the subject of lipstick, which, like so much of our modern makeup, dates back thousands of years. The earliest known pots of lip color were found in a burial tomb in an ancient city called Ur, in what is now southeastern Iraq. Dating from roughly 3000 B.C., these ancestors to our modern lipsticks were made from what must have been a truly unkissable concoction of crushed red rocks. We know, too, that the ancient Egyptians wore lip color at around the same time. They would grind up reddish plant dyes like henna and mix them with animal fats and oils to make them easier to paint on. Many Egyptian women also favored a bluish hue for their lips, which probably went quite well with the blue-black wigs we associate with these ancient people. These same women were often eventually entombed with little pots of makeup as well, for those much-needed afterlife touch-ups.

Some of the ingredients that centuries-old lipstick addicts had to contend with were truly stomach-turning – or worse. To get that "healthy" tinge, women smeared their lips with mixtures made from iron ore, lead, the sediment of red wine, the bodies of dead insects, and even a plant dye called fucus, which turned out to be a deadly poison. In the late 1500s, England's Queen Elizabeth I wore lip color that was a combination of cochineal (a dye extracted from a tiny sucking insect), egg whites, and fig milk.

In ancient Rome, women and men wore lip color; for the men, different hues indicated their rank in society.

As recently as the 1920s, lipstick was still being made from crushed bugs, beeswax, and olive oil, and it often went rancid mere hours after it was first put on.

Today, lipstick – a slightly less nauseating mix of ingredients that include fish scales, powdered pigments, waxes, and castor oil – is often called the most used cosmetic. In North America, somewhere between 75 and 95 percent of women say they wear it on a regular basis. Numbers are slightly lower in other Western nations, but lipstick sales still outnumber those of other cosmetics by a massive margin. Things weren't always this way, however. During the French Revolution, for example, lip color became associated with the aristocracy, and the act of wearing it was often enough to win a fine lady a trip to the guillotine. In the late 1700s, British women could be tried for witchcraft for wearing lipstick to bewitch men and trick them into marriage. The Victorians often denounced makeup of all kinds, but especially lipstick, as impolite and even deceitful.

This idea that women used lipstick to somehow misrepresent their true selves – by hiding their lack of natural beauty, perhaps, or even making themselves appear healthier than they actually were – appears with surprising frequency throughout history.

Makeup-wearers were constantly being accused of ensnaring, entrancing, and beguiling men who were apparently so disoriented by the sight of a woman with red-painted lips that they couldn't think straight. A 1915 law in Kansas made it a misdemeanor for any woman under the age of forty-four (!) to wear lipstick and other cosmetics to create "a false impression." A similar law in Pennsylvania gave husbands the right to annul their marriages if, unbeknownst to them, their wives had worn lipstick during their courtship.

These laws, mercifully, are off the books now, but lipstick continues to spark complicated reactions. We do wear it, like all makeup, to conceal or disguise, if only to a small degree, and most women who regularly wear lipstick say they wouldn't dream of leaving the house without having it on. And then there's the often contradictory attitude of men toward lipsticked women. Most will admit that the sight of a red-lipped lady is very alluring, but a majority also say that they don't like to kiss their girlfriends or wives if they're wearing lip color. One (male) writer even lamented "the billions and trillions of kisses that never happened because of that confounded red paste that women have been taught to smear upon their lips in the wackiest paradox of modern times."

M

Money

W e are close to living in what is called a cashless society. Many people have their paychecks deposited directly into their bank accounts without ever seeing or touching them. We can pay bills over the Internet, without needing to write checks, and we can buy products with credit cards (if we perhaps don't have the money to pay for them) or debit cards (if we do). It has taken us about 4,500 years of inventing and reinventing money to get to the point where we no longer need it at all.

Before someone came up with the idea of money, societies operated on the barter system, something that's still practiced in developing countries in many parts of the world. If you lived in a place without money and had to barter for the things you wanted to buy, you would have to have something useful to trade. Let's say you had your eye on a fetching pair of shoes, for example. You would need to find something the shoemaker was willing to trade for, either among the things you already owned or by trading with someone else for something you knew the shoemaker wanted. You could easily spend hours or days searching for just the item you needed. It was obviously not a very efficient way of doing business.

Some items were easier to barter with than others, however. Most everyone would accept things like cattle, cloth, and salt, so these became a kind of currency. In parts of Africa and Central and South America, iron and copper tools were also used as a unit of exchange. Like salt and cloth, these tools were immensely practical, so it was easy to convince people to accept them in trade. Eventually, someone thought to make smaller, more delicate replicas of hoes and knives and axes to stand in for the real thing. In a sense, these became the first coins.

Actual, minted coins developed out of the practice of using weighed metals as currency. Inscriptions from Mesopotamia, in what is now southern Iraq, show that people measured out amounts of silver to pay rents and taxes as early as 2500 B.C. Because the value of the payment was established by weight, the

She Sells Seashells

The amazing thing about money is that it can be anything a community values. In China, as early as about 1500 B.C., people exchanged shells from tiny sea snails called cowries for items they needed, and a pictograph of the cowrie shell and a fishing net was for a long time the Chinese symbol for trade. The cowrie shell remained in circulation in various parts of the world to the mid-twentieth century, making it easily the longest-used currency in history.

number of pieces turned over – and their size and shape – was irrelevant. Some people took to carrying around small, thin bits of silver wherever they went; pieces could be cut or broken off as needed to make unexpected purchases.

It was just a small step from there to the first real coins, and these were invented in a place called Lydia, in what is now Turkey, in the seventh century B.C. The coins were made from a metal called electrum, a naturally occurring mix of gold and silver, and they came in different weights (and therefore had different values). They were stamped with an emblem of a lion's head, the symbol of Lydian royalty, which confirmed that the value was as advertised. People knew instantly that any coin that didn't bear the lion's head was a forgery.

Like the ancient Lydians, we also stamp our coins with an emblem representing our head of state to confirm that they are authentic and have been issued by the government.

The real beauty of the Lydian coins, however, was that their value was stamped right on them, which meant that merchants and traders didn't have to perform the time-consuming task of weighing each coin to determine its worth. The benefits of this could not be denied, and other countries quickly began producing coins of their own.

Paper money, on the other hand, took a lot longer to catch on. By perhaps the 600s A.D., the Chinese had begun to tire of the pounds and pounds of heavy coins they were forced to lug around. People started to leave their coins with merchants – the first bankers, you could say – in exchange for handwritten receipts made out in the same amount; they could then hand these receipts on to other merchants to buy whatever they needed. Although they weren't issued by the government, these receipts were, in effect, paper money.

The explorer and trader Marco Polo brought this paper money to the attention of Europeans in the 1200s. But it took another four hundred years for the idea to catch on. Europeans couldn't grasp the concept of using paper, which has no value on its own, to *represent* money; coins at least were made of metals that were actually worth something, so the idea of assigning them a monetary value made sense.

Eventually, European banks began to issue notes – banknotes, a word we now use to refer to paper money in general – to their clients; these could be exchanged for gold and silver coins that were held by the banks in accounts. Account holders could write money orders for people they owed debts to, and these also could be turned in to the banks to be filled.

Any piece of written material that a society agreed to recognize could become a form of paper money. In the early days of the North American colonies, when no local banks had yet been established and currency (or the lack of it) was a constant problem, people got very creative. In 1685, the desperate governor of New France, whose shipments of money from the mother country were often delayed by poor weather, started paying the colony's soldiers in playing cards. Each card was given a certain value and signed by him to make it legal tender.

The Thirteen Colonies had a similar problem. England deliberately restricted the money supply there, to try to keep the colonists from trading with other countries. Most transactions were done with bills of exchange, which English merchants would accept but no one else would. The colonists soon tired of always being short of the things they needed, however, and they began bartering with Natives and traders from other nations using beaver pelts, tobacco, Native American wampum (beaded belts), and other things of value. From 1652 to 1682, the Massachusetts Bay Colony even minted its own silver coins. To get around a British law that said only the king could issue money, the colony dated all its coins 1652, a year when there was no monarch on the English throne.

> ## Shave and a Haircut – Two Bits
>
> Because there were so few British coins circulating in the Thirteen Colonies, coins of other nations were highly valued. The most plentiful were dollars from Spain called pieces of eight, which were minted from silver extracted from mines in Central and South America. These large coins could be chopped into eight pieces, or bits, to make change – two bits for a quarter of a dollar, four bits for half a dollar, and so on. This is why we still sometimes use the term "two bits" as a synonym for twenty-five cents.

Somewhere along the way, money was transformed from a way of acquiring things of value into something that we value for its own sake. People began to hoard money, and to admire those who had a lot of it more than those who had none. It was the wrong road to venture down – the love of money, after all, is supposed to be the root of all evil – and we were soon being warned, none too subtly, against the dangers of prizing money beyond all else. A mere thirty pieces of silver make Judas betray Jesus in the Bible. Greedy King Midas learns the downside of getting what you wish for when everything he touches, including his own children, turns to gold. Scrooge is shown the future of loneliness and misery that his own miserly ways are creating for him.

And yet money also has its virtues. Ancient shipbuilders summoned protection for their vessels by hiding a gold coin at the base of the mast. Today, we toss coins in fountains to make our wishes come true and believe found pennies will bring good fortune. (Coins that are spotted during a rainstorm are considered especially lucky because they are supposed to have fallen from heaven.) We give children money cards as birthday presents, and if we choose a wallet or a piggy bank as a gift, we try to remember to include a coin "for luck." In Britain, special coins called Maundy money are handed out to the poor every year on the Thursday before Easter, a tradition that dates back to at least the 1300s. Sometimes we even bury our dead with money – so they can buy their way into heaven, if they need to.

Every day, we come closer and closer to realizing a truly cash-less society. But that dream brings with it some complex problems. So-called digital money – money that is converted into a code and stored on a plastic card or in your computer's hard drive – is too tempting for many criminals to resist. Already we have seen web-sites breached and personal and credit card information stolen, and people fear that a clever hacker could eventually do the same to a digital cash system, wiping out the wealth of thousands in mere minutes. Yet with today's high-quality photocopiers, printers, and scanners, traditional money isn't much safer. Counterfeiting has become such a massive global problem that even the U.S. Treasury has been forced to redesign the American dollar, the most recog-nized (and most counterfeited) currency in the world. Modern security features employed by the American and other national governments include watermarks, raised printing, unique inks and paper, tiny security fibers, microprinting, and holograms and color-shifting inks that change tints as the money moves. In Australia, they have even experimented with plastic bills with clear windows that cannot be reproduced by photocopiers. Until we've actually attained that cashless society, it's good to know that there's more to our cash than meets the eye.

Numbers

The fear of the number thirteen is so widespread that we have coined a special term – triskaidekaphobia – to describe it. People the world over refuse to work on the thirteenth floor, live in house number 13, or make major decisions on the thirteenth of the month. A Friday that falls on the thirteenth is a worse omen to many people. Even those who claim not to be superstitious will avoid making significant purchases or traveling on Friday the thirteenth, and some refuse to show up for work. All told, triskaidekaphobia and its mouth-twisting counterpart, paraskevidekatriaphobia (fear of Friday the thirteenth), cost world economies billions of dollars a year.

One commonly held belief is that the fear of thirteen has its origins in the biblical Last Supper, whose thirteenth – and final – guest was Judas Iscariot, the betrayer of Christ. Certainly this is where we get another popular superstition – the belief that if you ever sit down to dinner with just twelve other people, one person at the table (usually the last to sit or the first to rise) will die within the year. But in fact there is some evidence that the fear of thirteen predates the Bible. The Romans considered it a symbol of death, and it's a supremely unlucky number in both Norse and Hindu mythology. In tarot decks, thirteen is the death card, and witches' covens usually have thirteen members.

Thirteen is not the only number believed to have magical properties, however. In the West, there are several so-called sacred numbers, and most of those do have some relationship to the Bible. Three, for instance, recalls the Holy Trinity; in modern life, we talk of three guesses and three wishes, of good things coming in threes, and of the third time being "the charm." Some of the Bible's sacred numbers take their cue from nature. Four, for example, represents not only the Christian cross and the four gospels, but also the four points on the compass, the four seasons of the year, and the four phases of the moon. Twelve is the number of Jesus' apostles, as well as the number of months of the year and hours in each half of the day. There are also twelve signs in the zodiac, which has important symbolism for cultures all over the world.

Perhaps the most universal of all "lucky" numbers is seven. In Japanese mythology, there were seven gods of good fortune. Native Americans believed in seven cosmic truths and medieval Christians in seven deadly sins. The Goths had seven gods, and in ancient times people thought there were seven planets in our solar system. We have seven days in the week, seven wonders in the world, and seven seas to cross. In literature, Sinbad makes seven voyages, Snow White has to contend with seven dwarfs,

The number four brings good luck in most countries – except China, where the word for "four," she, is uncomfortably close to shi, the word for "death."

and Harry Potter's story unfolds in seven volumes. Even Adolf Hitler thought seven had magical properties; he launched all his major offensives on the seventh of the month.

Ultimately, the belief in lucky and unlucky numbers is simply a superstition. Traditionally denounced by the church as the invention of the Devil or the product of paganism, most superstitions were born in eras when people were less enlightened and more likely to believe in magic and fate and powers beyond their control. The superstitions that have survived through to this day (many haven't) all have magical, mystical origins, although we often observe the superstition without knowing its history.

How many of us, for example, toss spilled salt over our left shoulder without realizing that we're doing so to scare away the Devil before he has a chance to whisper evil in our ear? Or touch or knock wood with no awareness that this is the way to summon pagan wood spirits? The taboo against walking under ladders has to do with the belief that the wall, the ladder, and the ground form a triangle representing the Holy Trinity; anyone who walks under a ladder is breaking the triangle and therefore showing disrespect for God. Broken mirrors bring bad luck because the first looking glasses were thought to have magical powers. People, it was believed, could ask a mirror questions and get glimpses of the future (think of Snow White), but if it shattered, that was a sign of impending doom.

Many superstitions began to lose their power with the dawn of the Age of Reason, or the Enlightenment, in the 1600s. Over the next two centuries, huge advances were made in medicine, chemistry, mathematics, and physics, and people began to depend less on luck and magic and more on intellect. These were the beginnings of our modern-day love of science and education, and our faith in things that we can see with our own eyes and touch with our own hands.

Some superstitions persist, however, no matter how rational and informed we become. In fact, recent studies have concluded that a belief in superstitions is on the rise in the West, with a 2003 British survey showing that a whopping 77 percent of people will admit to being at least a little superstitious. Most of us claim not to be part of that 77 percent, but we'll nevertheless walk around ladders, toss salt when we've upended the shaker, and cross the street to escape black cats. Superstition, it seems, is alive and well in the twenty-first century.

O

Oaths

Battered, half-starved, and having lost thousands of men in a hopeless campaign to win the American Civil War for the Confederate (southern) states, General Robert E. Lee wrote to Ulysses S. Grant, the leader of the Union (northern) armies, and asked what conditions he would place on Lee's surrender. The next day, April 8, 1865, Grant wrote back that, peace being his great desire, he would insist only that Lee and his men sign an oath promising never to take up arms again against the government of the United States.

On the morning of April 9, saying he would rather die a thousand deaths than do what he was about to, Lee – generally considered one of the greatest military men the United States has ever produced – sent Grant a white flag and a note of surrender. A few hours later, the two men met in the front parlor of a local home, where Lee signed a document that read, in part, "We, the undersigned, prisoners of war belonging to the Army of Northern Virginia, . . . do hereby give our solemn parole of honor that we will not hereafter serve the armies of the Confederate States, or in any military capacity whatever, against the United States of America." Lee and his men were allowed to keep their guns and even their horses, "for the spring plowing." Grant, so the story goes, did not so much as glance at the parole that Lee had signed. Instead, he handed the historic document to his military secretary and explained that Lee's word alone was good enough for him.

Paroles like the one signed by Lee have a long history in times of conflict. From the days of ancient Greece and Rome to the cusp of the twentieth century, prisoners of war were frequently let go having signed an oath – or simply recited one – saying they would not resume fighting against the forces that had captured them. A soldier's word was considered a binding contract.

Oaths like these belong to a time when language had more power than it does today. In centuries long since past, people would appeal to the gods to hear their promise or confirm the truthfulness of a statement. The force of the oath depended on the belief of all involved that the punishment for lying would be severe. The ancient Greeks, for example, were convinced that Zeus would strike down perjurers with a lightning bolt. With that kind of threat hovering in the air, no one, the theory went, would be foolish or arrogant enough to break a vow.

*The military parole of honor is the origin of our modern practice of granting well-behaved prisoners early release from jail. Just like the soldiers of old, prisoners give their word (*parole, *in fact, is French for* "word"*) to stay on the right side of the law in exchange for their freedom.*

Over time, oaths took on a kind of legal status. In medieval Europe, a person could often establish his innocence of a crime simply by swearing an oath and producing a set number of people who said they believed it. We see remnants of this tradition in our modern judicial system, where jury members are sworn in and witnesses take oaths before testifying (although today we need the threat of a perjury charge to ensure that they honor their word).

Medieval people were big on oaths of all kinds. Among the most common were what were called fealty oaths ("fealty" essentially means loyalty or fidelity). Under the feudal system, these oaths were used to bind a vassal to his lord. The vassal would pledge allegiance and promise to fight on the lord's behalf, and the lord, in turn, would vow to treat his vassal with honor. Once he'd made his oath, the vassal was given the rights to a fief (a parcel of land), an arrangement often symbolized by the lord's ceremoniously handing over a clump of dirt. As long as he respected his oath, the vassal was entitled to anything the fief, and the peasants working on it, produced.

The principle of fealty has survived into the present day in the form of loyalty oaths. Soldiers of most countries, for example, recite an oath promising to uphold their constitution or the laws of their state, and to protect their nation against all enemies. Elected officials, from presidents and prime ministers on down, usually swear a similar oath, often called an oath of office, and in the United States many schoolchildren pledge allegiance to their flag each day.

Modern oath-taking is not without controversy, however. The push to have children recite the Pledge of Allegiance has drawn many court challenges, including a famous one from the Jehovah's Witnesses, a group of conservative Christians who refused to swear an oath to anyone or anything other than God. A more recent court case charged that the pledge is unconstitutional because it includes the phrase "one nation under God," added in the 1950s to offset the supposed influence of "godless"

I Do Solemnly Swear

One of the few surviving professional pledges is the Hippocratic Oath. Administered to virtually all graduates of Western medical schools, this oath has been called one of the oldest binding documents in history.

Hippocrates, the man for whom the oath was named, was an ancient Greek physician who worked hard to take the superstition out of medicine and turn it into a science based on observation, logic, and reason. He urged his fellow physicians to lead honorable lives, and to place the needs of their patients before all else, principles that are reflected in the moral code doctors are expected to follow to this day.

The classical version of the Hippocratic Oath, written sometime around the 300s B.C., was recited to the god Apollo Physician and "all the gods and goddesses." It emphasized the need to keep patients from harm, prohibited doctors from using knives, and obligated them to value their mentors, even to the point of giving them money if they needed it. Today's version, rewritten to better represent the role of the physician in the modern world, stresses doctor–patient confidentiality, humility in the face of a physician's at times staggering responsibilities, and an awareness that "warmth, sympathy, and understanding may outweigh the surgeon's knife or the chemist's drug."

Communist spies. That phrase, lawyers argued, violates the principle of the separation of church and state, a cornerstone of the American constitution. Similar court cases have also challenged the constitutionality of forcing people to swear loyalty oaths. In the mid-1950s, the same fear of Communism that infiltrated the Pledge of Allegiance sparked a push for loyalty oaths at all levels of government and in many educational institutions, like universities. Employees had to affirm that they were not members of the Communist Party or any other organization bent on overthrowing the government. Those who refused were instantly fired, and many spent more than a decade fighting in the courts to regain their jobs.

With a few exceptions – like the oath of citizenship or the vows that brides and grooms exchange on their wedding day – oaths have largely lost their place in our modern world. Some of the language of oath-taking has survived, but it is now so overused that it doesn't carry the weight it once did. We may swear to God that we're telling the truth, for example, and ask that He strike us down if we're lying, but unlike our ancestors, we don't believe that will actually happen. Even the word "oath" is now more often used to mean a curse or profanity than a solemn vow. In a sign, perhaps, of how cheapened our language has become, the twenty-first-century oath-taker is more likely to swear *at* someone than *to* something.

P

Pretzels

Once elbowed aside by more popular snacks like potato chips and chocolate bars, the humble pretzel has, in recent years, been enjoying a small revival. Street vendors on the corners of many North American cities hawk warm, soft, chewy pretzels topped with salt and a special mustard or, for the more adventurous, butter, cheese, or chocolate. Even the small, hard, store-bought pretzel – now often sourdough or multigrain, shaped into sticks, twists, nuggets, or nibblers – is finding new admirers.

According to legend, pretzels were invented in the 600s by a monk who killed an afternoon twisting strips of dough until they looked like a person's arms crossed in prayer. (The word "pretzel" comes from *bracciatelli*, the Italian for "folded arms.") When he showed his fellow monks what he had created, they decided the baked dough would make a nice reward for any children who performed well in their religious studies. They also used the three distinct segments of the pretzel to help children understand the concept of the Holy Trinity.

The pretzel was a great success, and soon it became an important Christian symbol of unity and spirituality. For a time, it was also believed to bring prosperity and good fortune; brides and grooms would break a pretzel on their wedding day, as we do the wishbone of the Thanksgiving turkey, and then eat the pieces as a gesture of their commitment to each other.

Perhaps because of their associations with spirituality and religious devotion, pretzels were a favorite food to eat in many parts of Europe during Lent, the forty-day period leading up to Easter.

In one New Year's Day tradition, German children in North America hung pretzels from their necks with string to summon good fortune for the year ahead.

At one time, fasting and self-sacrifice were a big part of the Lenten season, and pretzels were among the few foods considered acceptable to eat. Starting on Ash Wednesday, vendors would peddle their wares, working straight through until Easter Sunday to distribute their salty treats to the most devout. In Germany, children would search for pretzels that their parents had hidden under bushes and in straw bales, a precursor to the modern Easter egg hunt. Pretzels were also handed out to the hungry and the poor, not just during Lent but all year round. Those who donated their time to feed the less fortunate in this way were looked upon by other Christians as especially saintly; some were buried with pretzels in their coffins to help them make their way to heaven without delay.

Pretzels also apparently played a role in repelling a Turkish attack on Vienna in the early sixteenth century. It seems that the would-be invaders were unable to scale the city's walls and instead decided to tunnel their way in. The noise they made as they tried to burrow through the ground was heard by pretzel bakers who were working all night on their stock for the next morning. They notified the guards, the city was saved, and to this day many European bakers use the pretzel as a symbol of their brave and honorable profession.

Q

Queen's English

T he English language, now spoken by about half a billion people worldwide, was actually brought to England by invaders from northern Germany. In the mid-fifth century A.D., three seafaring tribes – the Angles, the Jutes, and the Saxons – saw their chance to fill the void left by departing Roman soldiers and launched their own assault on the southern and eastern coasts of England (or "the land of the Angles"). The language they carried with them across the cold and stormy North Sea developed into Old English, then Middle English, and finally Modern English, the most widely used language in the world.

English is often accused of being an impossibly complicated language, horribly difficult for non-native speakers to learn. It is full of words like "eight" and "enough" and "feign," which look as if they should be pronounced something like *ey-get*, *en-oog*, and *fi-gen*, but of course are not. In fact, though, people who study languages tell us that about 84 percent of English words are entirely straightforward and get pronounced exactly as they seem they should. Another 13 percent follow the rules closely enough that most people can sound them out without making too many mistakes. The problems lie in the final 3 percent, a small but troublesome group of words that don't behave in any predictable fashion and simply have to be committed to memory. Unfortunately for anyone trying to learn the language, that 3 percent includes four hundred of our most commonly used words, such as "of," "four," "done," and "love."

English is probably the world's most well-documented language, and this is one reason why so many illogical spellings have survived through to the present day. People began producing English-language dictionaries almost as soon as the printing press was invented in Europe, in the 1400s (see the entry on Xeroxing), and these dictionaries fixed, perhaps for all time, many of the spellings that make the least sense to us today.

Over the past four centuries or so, a number of people have argued for the simplification of English spellings. One of them, Noah Webster, the creator of the 1828 *American Dictionary of the English Language*, was successful enough in his efforts that, to this day, Britons and Americans spell many words differently (with Canadians, as always, trying to occupy a neutral middle ground). Webster gave the world -*or* spellings instead of -*our* (favor/favour), -*er* instead of -*re* (center/centre), and -*yze* instead of -*yse* (analyze/analyse). He also introduced many phonetic spellings – that is, spellings based on how words sound – including "skeptical" (for "sceptical"), "plow" (for "plough"), and "check" (for "cheque"). One theory is that

"Queen's English" is a term we use to refer to the language as it is properly spoken and written in Britain. Unless some unthinkable disaster strikes, the next British monarch will be male, and the term will soon become "King's English."

Webster hoped to make the language more rule-abiding so that Americans, who tended to have less formal education, could more easily learn to read and write.

But Webster was, by all accounts, a grim, miserable man, and in the end, he was not able to talk people around to accepting some of his more radical changes, like spelling "women" as *wimmen* and "tough" as *tuf*. He learned that the more common a word is, the greater the resistance to changing it. There's hardly an English-speaker on earth who won't, for example, oppose spelling "of" as *ov*, whether it makes more sense or not.

We hang on to many of our oddest spellings because, for one thing, they reflect the English language's far-reaching linguistic

Could You Repeat That?

Despite its small size and its geographic isolation, Great Britain has the widest variety of dialects (styles of speaking specific to certain regions, like distinct accents) in the English-speaking world. Experts can't agree on the total number, but it seems to be somewhere between a dozen and as many as forty.

Dialects can often reveal a wealth of information about people, from their place of birth to their occupation to, of course, their class and level of education. In war-torn Northern Ireland, dialects differ between Catholics and Protestants, and have reportedly been used by the Irish Republican Army to determine the fate of captives. In England, where dialects are often especially noticeable, some people claim to be able to tell not only what village someone hails from but whether he was born on the north or south side of the town's main street.

ancestry. Though it began life as a Germanic dialect, English has, over 1,500 years, picked up influences from all over the world. It is estimated, for instance, that when the Normans ruled England, from 1066 to 1154, they introduced ten thousand French-derived words into the language, a full three-quarters of which we still use today. We have also borrowed freely from Latin, Greek, Danish, Swedish, Spanish, and even Russian. In fact, many people have argued that one of the great strengths of English is its willingness to embrace words from just about anywhere. We adopt, without translation, terms like "macho," "kindergarten," "maître d'," and, more recently, "smorgasbord" and "glasnost." This gives our language a richness and an inclusiveness that others sometimes lack. (Although English, of course, has repaid the favor, infiltrating languages all over the globe, and sometimes creating hybrid monsters like Denglish, a mix of German and English, and Franglais, a mix of English and French.)

Today, most language experts agree that there are about 200,000 English words in everyday use. (French makes do with roughly half that number.) With a language so vast, we can often be more precise with meaning than non-English speakers, distinguishing between, for example, "earth" and "ground," "house" and "home," "story" and "history." And the language continues to grow and evolve, transforming itself to meet the requirements of an ever-changing world. When the first English-language dictionaries were published, they listed about 3,000 words. Samuel Johnson's landmark *Dictionary of the English Language*, published in 1755, contained 43,000 words, and the granddaddy of them all, the *Oxford English Dictionary*, has a mind-boggling 615,000. When you add all the scientific, medical, and technical terms that don't get included in dictionaries meant for the general public, you're probably talking about many millions of words, with perhaps tens of thousands more being coined with each passing year.

R

Rice

In 1787, the future American president Thomas Jefferson, then ambassador to France, traveled to Italy on a mission to discover the secret behind the Italians' great-tasting rice. The British had made off with South Carolina's entire rice crop, including the seed needed for replanting, during the American Revolution, and Jefferson was bent on bringing his country's rice industry back to life. Alas, the Italians kept the mysteries of their crop well hidden, so Jefferson had to resort to some trickery to get what he wanted. "I am determined to take enough to put you in seed," he wrote to a friend back in the now empty Carolina rice fields. "They informed me, however, that its exportation in the husk was prohibited, so I could only bring out as much as my coat and surtout pockets would hold."

When Jefferson scampered out of Italy, his pockets bulging with his pilfered grains, he did help salvage the economically important American rice industry. But despite its value as a staple crop, rice is not native to North America, having been brought here in the late 1600s in ships from Madagascar, an island east of Africa. The Madagascans had themselves been introduced to rice by some tireless people from the island of Java, in Indonesia, who'd paddled their outrigger canoes across thousands of miles of ocean to bring the special grain to their island friends.

Rice is an incredibly ancient grain. Scientists believe its ancestry can be traced back 100 million years, to Gondwanaland, the giant land mass that eventually broke apart to form Africa, Antarctica, Australia, and South America. It has been cultivated – that is, grown deliberately as a source of food, instead of left to grow wild – since about 5000 B.C. People in southern China, Laos, Thailand, and Vietnam were the first to figure out how to raise it as a crop, and from there it quickly spread north to Korea, south to Indonesia, and west to India, all places where rice remains a staple to this day.

North American wild rice is in fact a grass plant not closely related to rice. Traditionally, Native Americans harvested it by bending the towering stalks over the side of their canoes and beating them with sticks to knock the grains free.

Originally rice was thought of as a dry-land plant, but eventually farmers realized that it grew faster and more abundantly in water. This was not as happy a discovery as you might think, for it's no easy feat to keep a plant submerged. Those early farmers had to learn to flatten their fields, build retaining walls, and find some way to get water on and off their land – which often just meant waiting for the rainy season to come and go, but sometimes involved constructing aqueducts and dikes and drainage systems. In the mountains of the Philippines, you can still see rice terraces that date back two or three thousand years and were built by hand with only the most primitive tools. Today villagers continue to harvest the rice and maintain the terraces as others did centuries ago.

Any crop as old as rice is bound to inspire the imagination. From the Philippines to China to India, myths about its origins tell of beautiful maidens who meet tragic ends, only to sprout rice plants from their graves. Other stories center around brave heroes who storm heaven and steal the secret grain for the benefit of humankind, just as, in the Greek myths, Prometheus snatches fire from the gods. In still others, the rice pot is like Pandora's box; it will produce endless quantities of rice as long as no one ever looks inside, which of course someone inevitably does. In Pandora's story, human curiosity unleashes disease, sorrow, and misfortune on the world. When the lid of the rice pot is lifted, it's hard labor that's set loose.

These stories all share the conviction that rice is a gift of the gods. It is no surprise, then, that it is also commonly associated with prosperity, good fortune, and fertility. In Hindu weddings, the bridal couple will be showered with rice grains to ensure a long marriage with many children. (We echo this custom in the West when we toss handfuls of rice at the bride and groom as they leave the church.) In China, knocking over your rice bowl is an incredibly bad omen, and it's also thought to be bad luck – and just plain rude – to leave any grains uneaten at the bottom of your dish.

In most rice-growing cultures, elaborate ceremonies go along with the planting and harvesting of the grain. People consult fortune-tellers to learn what day to plant on and even what clothes to wear while they do the sowing. At harvest time, women often go into the fields to collect a few stalks to make into a rice doll, which is then given pride of place in the family's granary. (This doll will guarantee that there is plenty of fertile seed for the next year's crop.) As a general rule, all rice that is harvested is hulled and cooked far from the paddies it came from. The grain is viewed as a living, feeling being, and the knowledge of the fate that awaits her in our cooking pots must be kept from her for as long as possible.

Rice sustains more than half the people on the planet. The Japanese roll it into balls called *onigiri*, the Italians simmer it into risotto, the Spanish add saffron and chicken to make paella, people in India mix it with spicy seasonings and meats for biryani and pilaf, and the English add raisins and cook it up into sweet rice pudding. Today, over a billion people spend their lives growing and harvesting rice, in fact, and many of them still raise the crop in much the same way as their ancestors did.

S

Sideburns

The American Civil War general Ambrose Burnside was not much of a soldier. Indecisive, lacking in confidence, and given to hatching some pretty baffling schemes to get the better of the rebel troops he was fighting against, he lost almost every battle he took part in. He trapped his men on a narrow stone bridge with the enemy waiting at the other end, bogged them down in mud so thick it actually drowned some of the horses, and caught them in a massive, steep-sided crater he himself had blown into the landscape.

You'd think a man like that was best forgotten, but we remember Ambrose Burnside to this day — not for his military genius, of course, but for his grooming habits. Although Burnside may have been a flop as a soldier, he was a tall, impressive-looking man, with huge, bushy whiskers that stretched down from his ears and joined up with his mustache. They were such a signature feature that people named them in his honor, christening them not burnsides but sideburns.

Facial hair was an absolute must for men in Burnside's day, especially in the military. Beards were thought to be more manly, more natural, and even better for the wearer's health than a clean-shaven face. Soon the trend caught on with writers and artists, politicians and businessmen. On the eve of the 1860 American presidential election, a young girl wrote to one beardless candidate to tell him that he'd better get growing if he wanted to take over the White House. "All the ladies like whiskers," she informed him, "and they would tease their husbands to vote for you" – most American women didn't get the vote until the early 1900s – "and then you would be President." The skeptical Abraham Lincoln took her advice and soon after won the day.

Young soldiers who couldn't quite muster a mustache often painted on a fake one until Mother Nature came to the rescue.

If he were alive today, Ambrose Burnside would no doubt be relieved to find that his name is linked to facial hair rather than to military ineptitude. "Eponyms" are what we call words that are drawn from the names of real people, and English has literally hundreds of them. The sandwich, for instance, was named for John Montague, the Earl of Sandwich, an English nobleman who was such an incurable gambler that he asked a servant to make him a portable meal of sliced meat between two pieces of bread so he didn't have to leave the card table to eat. Amelia Bloomer is one of the few females we remember in an eponym. An early activist for women's voting rights, Bloomer argued for more practicality in female dress and gave her name to bloomers, loose-fitting pants that were about as functional as clothes got for women during the Victorian era.

Bloomer and the Earl of Sandwich may have enjoyed their notoriety, but some people would probably have preferred to slip into anonymity than to be remembered the way they are. Charles Lynch was an eighteenth-century Virginia farmer who had a fondness for taking the law into his own hands. He gave his name to those out-of-control crowds we call lynch mobs, and to the term "lynching," putting someone to death without first having a trial.

The Reverend William Archibald Spooner was a brilliant scholar and clergyman, but he was also a bit of a nervous Nellie. In his lectures and sermons, he apparently had an unfortunate habit of mixing up the first letters of some of his words, resulting in hilarious miscues like "You have hissed my mystery lectures" and "We all know what it is to have a half-warmed fish inside us." Today we call these slips of the tongue (or, as Spooner might have said, "tips of the slung") spoonerisms.

When Dr. Joseph Guillotin stood up in the French revolutionary assembly and recommended a fancy new beheading machine to help dispatch traitors and other enemies of the state, his name quickly became linked with the truly horrendous device that we still call the guillotine. Interestingly, Dr. Guillotin was actually morally opposed to the death penalty; he hoped the adoption of what was supposed to be a more merciful means of execution would eventually lead to the abolition of the practice altogether.

But history has perhaps been most unkind to John Duns Scotus. This brilliant thirteenth-century thinker produced several great works of philosophy and logic, and he inspired a group of like-minded followers who called themselves Dunsmen. Unfortunately, he was also stubborn and a little out of touch with the times. Worst of all, he promoted the use of a bizarre cone-shaped hat – like a wizard's cap – that he claimed somehow increased the wearer's capacity for learning. Today, alas, we remember this hard-working, thoughtful man with a time-honored symbol of stupidity – the dunce cap.

Tulips

I t's a curious fact that we always act more foolishly in groups
than we do as individuals. Indeed, we've even coined a term
to describe those who unthinkingly join mass movements,
calling them lemmings, for those small, mouse-like rodents that,
according to legend, band together every few years and march off
to the sea to drown themselves.

Over the centuries, we have seen lemming-like behavior time
and again – the burning of accused witches in the Thirteen
Colonies in the 1690s, the persecution of supposed Communists
in 1950s North America, and most recently, the craze for "dot-
com" stocks that soon plunged investors into bankruptcy. Some
have called these passing manias "moral epidemics," and usually
they are driven by either fear or greed, and sometimes both.
It's as if whole cities or even nations go mad all at once, with

the citizens regaining their sanity only one person at a time.

One of the strangest of all these mass hysterias happened in Holland in the 1630s. Called tulipomania, it centered around those pretty, graceful flowers that brighten parks and private gardens all over the world.

We associate tulips with Holland even today – the tulip business is a major industry for the Dutch, and they export many billions of bulbs a year – but actually the flower came to that country from Constantinople (now Istanbul, Turkey), in the late 1500s. In fact, the name "tulip" comes from the Turkish word for "turban," and if you use your imagination, you can see a tiny turban in the shape the blossom takes.

At the height of the craze, tulips were so valuable that women wore them in their hair or hanging from their necks in place of jewelry.

Because of its novelty, the newly arrived tulip quickly became the most sought-after bloom in Holland. All people of wealth and influence had to have tulip beds in their gardens, and the flower was soon a status symbol, a sign of a person's rank and importance. By 1634, the entire nation had become so obsessed with tulips that even ordinary working people – carpenters and chimney sweeps and maidservants – were forsaking their regular duties to try to make their fortunes buying and selling bulbs.

The hysteria was fueled by the cultivation of new and rare varieties of bulbs. The most delicate flowers were of course the most prized, and one writer observed that when the tulip "has been weakened by cultivation, it becomes more agreeable in the eyes of the florist. . . . The more beautiful it turns, [it] grows so much the weaker, so that with the greatest skill and most careful attention, it can scarcely be transplanted, or even kept alive."

Solid-colored tulips were soon passé, and people wanted flowers of two or more colors. Called breaks – because they "broke" into unexpected patterns – these rare tulips would bloom solid one year and multicolored the next. (We now realize that this was caused by a virus, though the seventeenth-century Dutch growers had no way of knowing that.) There was even a sort of hierarchy of beauty among the breaks: varieties that broke into red and white or purple and white were the most prized, followed by those that broke into red and yellow, and finally those that were red or purple with a white border.

It was impossible to predict which bulbs would break and which would not, and that was much of the attraction. Of every hundred tulips cultivated in exactly the same way, only one, on average, would break. People bought great quantities of bulbs, gambling that the order would contain at least one break; if it did, it was like winning the lottery. Broken varieties were much more likely to produce offshoots that would themselves break, so the lucky owners could sell their bulbs to others for huge profits.

The varieties that had the potential to break into the most desired colors commanded the highest prices. One, known as *Semper Augustus*, rose from an already pricey 1,000 florins (the Dutch currency) to as much as 13,000 florins at the height of the frenzy. At the time, the average annual wage was about 150 florins and the finest houses in Amsterdam cost about 10,000. Although it's hard to compare currencies so many centuries apart, 13,000 florins would probably be more than a million dollars in today's money.

With so much at stake, it's no wonder that those who, through carelessness or defiance, disrespected the tulip bulb found themselves in quite a bit of hot water. One famous incident revolved around a poor sailor who brought word to a rich merchant of the arrival of a valuable shipment of goods. To thank him, the merchant went off to fetch the sailor a herring for his breakfast. While he was gone, the seaman saw what he thought was a common onion and decided to pocket it – having a particular fondness for onions with his herring. After he left, the merchant discovered the theft of what was in fact his priceless *Semper Augustus* tulip bulb, and he gave chase, his servants and assistants following in his frantic wake. They arrived at the dockside just in time to see the hapless sailor polishing off the last of what must have been a strange-tasting "onion." The horrified merchant eventually recovered his senses just enough to have the sailor charged with theft and locked away for the better part of a year!

In the end, inevitably, the bottom fell out of the tulip market and countless people were left holding the bulbs. Like most similar crazes, tulipomania was, at heart, a question of supply and demand. As soon as there were more sellers than buyers – more supply than demand – the collapse was unavoidable. Growers who had spent months cultivating bulbs for specific buyers found that their clients had changed their minds and were refusing to pay. Worse yet, some buyers had mortgaged their homes and businesses for a product that was no longer worth even a fraction of what they'd paid.

Having cost fortunes and ruined lives, the lowly bulb began the long, slow climb from scandal back to respectability. It has never again come close to the prices it achieved in the 1630s, which is just as well because, in those days, it was valued more for the money it could fetch than for its beauty. Still, tulipomania did awaken an interest in the flower among people outside Holland. Most Dutch growers were able to turn their attention to other countries after the collapse of the domestic tulip market, and that gave birth to an export business that still thrives almost four centuries later. Today there are about six thousand varieties of tulips, more than half of Holland's land mass is covered in bulb fields, and the flower has become a worldwide symbol of peace and co-operation between nations.

19th Century   21st Century

CALVIN KLEIN

Underwear

E ver since Adam and Eve discovered modesty and decided to cover themselves with fig leaves, people have been wearing undergarments. Centuries-old frescoes show ancient Greek women with lengths of cloth or leather strapped across their chests like modern-day brassieres, and even the five-thousand-year-old Iceman, freed from glacial captivity in the Italian Alps, was found with a loincloth and a fine pair of leather leggings.

For the ancients, underwear was probably worn mostly for extra warmth under their free-flowing togas and tunics. Decency may also have been a factor, since a rogue wind would have left little to any onlooker's imagination. Women – then as now – sometimes wore undergarments to flatten their stomachs and accentuate or conceal their breasts (depending on the fashion). Underwear probably did not need to play the crucial role it later would in maintaining personal hygiene, however; we know, from the evidence of their communal baths, their aqueducts, and their waste-disposal systems, that the early Greeks and Romans were a remarkably clean people for their time.

The same, unfortunately, cannot be said for those who lived during a period we often call the Dark Ages (from about 450 to 900 A.D.), when most of the knowledge people had acquired in those ancient, culturally advanced societies was lost. Hygiene, like so many other things, suffered greatly, for with no access to running water or public bathhouses, people washed themselves only rarely. Their undergarments became a sort of flimsy barrier between their filthy clothes and their equally filthy skin. Constructed from leather and bone, underthings were often worn until they literally disintegrated, without ever being washed. The potential for disease was enormous, and odors were barely masked by the oils and perfumes that were so freely applied.

Even as Western societies advanced in other ways, hygiene was slow to follow. It wasn't until the late 1700s that a French scientist devised a way to make soap in quantities and at prices that made it affordable to all. Soon, other technologies also came to the rescue. In 1793, Eli Whitney invented his famous cotton gin, making possible lightweight and easy-to-wash cotton undergarments. And with the dawn of the Industrial Revolution and the invention of the sewing machine in the 1800s, inexpensive, mass-produced underwear became a reality for all. Gone at last were the days of wearing your drawers until they fell to pieces around you.

The history of underwear – at least where women are concerned – is something like a miniature version of the history of Western society. The staid, constricting Victorian era, for example, produced corsets so tight that women could hardly breathe and frequently had difficulty moving around. By contrast, the First World War, which took women into the workforce in massive numbers and helped them gain the vote, introduced the world to the often braless flapper, a modern free spirit who liked loose dresses, bobbed hair, fast automobiles, and dances like the Charleston. The Depression-plagued 1930s and ultra-conservative 1950s saw the rise of the stifling girdle and the stiff crinoline, while the free-and-easy, countercultural 1960s resulted in braless women appealing to others to "let it all hang out."

For men, things were much simpler. In fact, in some ways it is only a short hop from the loincloth of old to the briefs they wear today. With the exception of an ill-advised excursion into male corsets in the early 1800s – and the occasional "stomacher" to corral an out-of-control waistline – men have preferred to keep their underthings practical and uncomplicated. The payoff has been much greater ease of movement than women enjoyed. Proof of this can be found in the close relationship between sports and men's underwear, with boxers and jockey shorts, for instance, taking their names from – you guessed it! – boxers and jockeys. Even those cold-weather favorites, long johns, have a sports connection. They were named for John L. Sullivan, a famous nineteenth-century heavyweight champion who liked to sport a pair of ankle-length woolen drawers whenever he climbed in the boxing ring.

Once she'd finished pulling on her chemise, corset, corset covers, and crinolines, a Victorian woman was often bound up in close to a dozen different undergarments.

We call our undergarments "unmentionables," and for most of human history that's exactly what they were. This was "intimate apparel," and you didn't discuss it with – or show it to – just anyone. But despite its associations with modesty, virtue, and morality, underwear – revealed to others only at the most private moments – has also always been bound up with sexuality and passion. When women of the 1960s began unhooking their bras and wriggling out of their girdles as a symbol of their newfound and hard-won liberation, underwear at last came out of the linen closet. It's now a fixture of our every-day lives – whether it's masquerading as outerwear on a fashion runway or peeking out over a waistband on Main Street – never to be unmentionable again.

Valentines

I n third-century Rome, a decidedly cruel emperor named
Claudius II banned marriage on the grounds that single men
made better, braver soldiers than those with wives and children.
According to legend, a local priest defied the unjust law and
continued to marry young couples in secret. The priest, called
Valentinus (or Valentine), was eventually found out, and Claudius
ordered him put to death for his "crime." Before his beheading,
however, Valentinus fell in love with the jailer's daughter, and on
the eve of his execution, which was to take place on February 14,
270 A.D., he sent her a love letter signed "From your Valentine."
This, supposedly, is the origin of our modern celebration of love,
Valentine's Day.

The unapologetically romantic Valentinus, who gave his life
for the love of others and finally found love himself on the verge

of death, was the perfect foil for the cold and heartless Claudius –
so much so that many people find his tale just a little too con-
venient. Some claim that the story of Valentine was invented by
church leaders because they needed a mid-February feast to
replace a festival called Lupercalia. Just as they would later do with
Samhain (see the entry on jack-o'-lanterns), Christians wanted

---

The Feast of Lupercalia

In ancient Rome, February 15 was a feast day
dedicated to the she-wolf, or *lupa*, who had raised
Romulus and Remus, the city's mythical founders.
Roman priests known as Luperci would gather each
year at the mouth of the cave where the twin boys
were supposed to have been reared. They would
sacrifice a goat, symbolizing fertility, and then cut its
hide into strips. Roman boys would take these strips,
dipped in the goat's sacrificial blood, and run through
the streets of the city, slapping local women as they
sprinted past. This was meant to purify (for which the
Latin word was *februa*, giving us the name of the
month) and to insure fertility, so the women were
more delighted than repulsed. They even believed this
gruesome ritual would make childbirth easier.

Later that same day, the unmarried women of
Rome would place their names, and perhaps also
little love notes, into a large urn. One at a time,
single Roman men drew out these names and, in this
way, chose the women they would be paired with for
the coming year. That's how Lupercalia, long before
Valentine's Day, became a festival celebrating love
and romance.

to create a church-approved holiday to stand in for the pagan feast that had existed before.

People began to mark what we now think of as Valentine's Day sometime in the 1600s, although the oldest surviving valentine – sent by a duke imprisoned in the Tower of London – dates back much further, to 1415. The holiday reached its peak, not surprisingly, during the strait-laced Victorian era, when it was considered inappropriate for people to openly express their feelings. Valentine cards were a safe way for young couples to show affection.

The symbolism of Valentine's Day is easy to decipher. The heart, pumping and passionate, is seen as the center of our emotional life, the opposite of our cool, rational minds, and so represents all our feelings, especially love. Cupid, the Roman god of love, stands poised with his bow and arrow, ready to intervene with those whose romantic lives need a little nudge. Flowers are a symbol of fertility, and red roses were the favorites of Venus, the Roman goddess of love and Cupid's mother. Other symbols, like rings and love-knots, represent unity and eternity, while birds signify partnership because, according to tradition, they choose the middle of February to begin mating.

Despite its Italian origins, Valentine's Day – carried to Britain by Roman soldiers – has always been most popular in the English-speaking world. Some early British valentine traditions even mimicked the Lupercalia festival. One widely practiced custom, for instance, dictated that the first young man a girl encountered on February 14 would become her boyfriend for that year, a clear echo of the drawing of lots of ancient times. In France, they did something similar, with village elders pairing up all the eligible bachelors and bachelorettes in town. If a girl was rejected by her intended suitor, she would hide herself away for eight days, waiting to take her revenge at a huge local bonfire, when the snobbish would-be lover would be burned in effigy while townspeople shouted insults at his likeness.

These customs were ripe for abuse, however, especially when left in the hands of mischievous elders who found it funny to pair up the most unlikely couples. By 1776, many French politicians had had enough; Parliament tried, with varying degrees of success, to outlaw the holiday, and it has only recently started to be celebrated openly again.

Today, thanks to the relentless efforts of greeting card companies, florists, and chocolatiers, Valentine's Day is more popular than ever. People send about a billion valentine cards a year, and the holiday has spread even to places like Mexico and Japan (where only women give valentine gifts, with the men reciprocating a month later, on a unique occasion known as White Day). Valentine's Day is also now the only saint's feast day that no longer has anything to do with the church, and while we may enjoy it simply as a wonderful celebration of romance, we've unfortunately almost forgotten the man it is meant to honor, locked away in his prison cell with only the jailer's daughter to love.

W

White

If black is the color of darkness and doom (see the entry on black), then white, its opposite, must represent innocence, purity, and hope. Black magic, used to conjure evil spirits, can be countered with white magic, used only for good. We tell white lies when we don't want to hurt someone's feelings, and we raise white flags of surrender when we want to lay down our arms and bring the killing to an end.

In the Western world, white is usually the color of weddings. A bride in a long white gown is the picture of virtue, and the couple's innocent hopes for the future are expressed in the towering white wedding cake, the reception dinner's pristine white place cards and floral centerpieces, and even the white rice that guests toss at the newlyweds to bring them luck.

White is clean and sterile, the traditional color of lab coats and nurses' uniforms. In the military, officers often give the troops' barracks "the white glove test," running their hands along every surface to see if even a speck of dust will be picked up by the immaculate white cotton fingers. White is impossible to keep clean without hours of vigilant attention, and that's why the color is associated with wealth, too – in the form of white-tie dinners, white-aproned maids, and tables set with crisp white napkins and tablecloths. For centuries, even pale white skin was a mark of upper-class status. Women painted and powdered their faces with wheat or rice flour, egg whites, or poisonous lead to achieve the wan complexion that said they whiled away the hours indoors, not toiling outside in the hot sun and wind. We even say that office workers and professionals are "white-collar," a reference to the dress shirts men typically wore with their jackets

Getting the Lead Out

For centuries, workers in paint factories risked being poisoned to the point of madness or death by the lead used to make most white paints. The process involved floating lead shavings in a bowl of vinegar and waiting until a chemical reaction had left a residue of white powder called lead carbonate. The paint workers would then pound this powder and mold it into small cakes, and it was the dust from this activity that so endangered their health. Even artists who used the paints to lighten and brighten their canvases were at risk. Many people speculate that lead poisoning caused the depression and black, black moods that drove Vincent van Gogh to cut off his ear and eventually kill himself.

and ties, of course, but also a holdover from the days when we wanted to distinguish the educated middle classes from their less fortunate blue-collar brothers.

We like to see the color white in our fairy tales, too, where it represents goodness in a sometimes harsh and cruel world. Alice goes through the looking-glass and comes face to face with not only the White Rabbit but also the White Queen and the White Knight. Dorothy gets swept away to the land of Oz, where Glenda the Good Witch, in her sparkling white gown, gives her the magic ruby slippers that will eventually let her find her way home. The Seven Dwarfs come home from work and find that their little house in the woods has been invaded by a beautiful girl whose skin is as white as snow.

But white isn't all wholesome innocence. If someone has been shocked or frightened, we'll often say he goes white as a sheet, and when we're in a rage we just can't control, our anger is described as white hot. White also suggests skeletons and bloodlessness. To intimidate enemy tribesmen, primitive warriors sometimes used chalk and powdered limestone to whiten their skin like bleached bones. White is the color of both angels and ghosts.

Most of all, though, white says cleanliness, hope, and the beginning of things. In 1792, when the American founding fathers began building a home suitable for the leader of their new nation, they decided it would have to be as white as the pure, elegant structures of that other great cradle of democracy, Greece. It took about a hundred tons (roughly 90,000 kilograms) of crushed lime to make the White House white, recreating the look, and thus the symbolism, of that celebrated ancient society. When archeologists later began to speculate that perhaps the famed buildings of Greece had not originally been white at all, but rather had been brightly painted with reds and blues and golds, people were alarmed. In one old joke, two archeologists are studying the ruins of a Greek temple. "Do you find any traces of color?" one asks his partner, who has climbed up for a closer look at a bit of molding. When his colleague says yes, the first archeologist is horrified. "Good Lord! Come down at once," he commands, glancing over his shoulder to make sure no one has overheard. How utterly unthinkable for the shrines of democracy to have been anything but pure, pristine white!

X

Xeroxing

There is a famous saying that necessity is the mother of invention. This was certainly true in the case of Chester Carlson, the inventor of xerography. A patent clerk for a New York City manufacturer of electrical parts, Carlson was plagued by eye problems and arthritis that made it difficult for him to copy out by hand all the patent applications, diagrams, and specifications sheets he dealt with every day. Convinced that there had to be a better way, he dreamed up a machine "that could be right in an office where you could bring a document to it, push it in a slot, and get a copy out." He began experimenting in the kitchen of his apartment with methods for duplicating documents using dry powder and static electricity. In late October 1938, after almost a decade of tedious and often smelly experiments, he made his first successful copy.

Carlson was one in a long line of men who gave their lives over to reproducing the written word to make it easier to preserve information and spread it to others. That line stretches all the way back to the Middle Ages, when monks toiled away in the isolation of their monasteries, copying out the few books, especially the Bible and works of religious history, that had survived the Dark Ages. These dedicated men, among the few people of that time who could read and write, also made their books easier to understand. While the Roman practice had been to write only in capital letters and to run all the words together, the scribes of the Middle Ages introduced lowercase letters, basic punctuation, and spaces to show where one word ended and another began. The documents they made, often decorated with beautiful, complicated designs in vivid colors and real gold leaf, were so bright that people started calling them illuminated manuscripts.

The scribes worked tremendously hard to safeguard books that might otherwise have been lost in those turbulent times. But their manuscripts were so elaborate and the cost of producing them so high that very few people had access to them. As the Middle Ages progressed and Europe, in particular, began to enjoy more prosperity, the demand for affordable books grew. More people were learning how to read and write, and there was a new thirst for knowledge.

Like many others of the time, a German goldsmith named Johann Gutenberg believed that there had to be an easier way to produce multiple copies of documents. In fact, the Chinese had already solved the problem, centuries earlier. They would take a page of text or pictures, carve the images in reverse into a block of wood, spread the block with ink, and press it onto paper (another Chinese invention) to make a duplicate. This was quicker and simpler than what those medieval monks were doing, but it still left a lot to be desired. For each new page to be copied, someone had to carve a whole new wood block from scratch, and if an error crept into the carving, the whole block had to be scrapped and the entire process repeated. Also, the wood blocks wore down with use, so even the ones that were properly carved could provide only a limited number of copies.

Gutenberg thought he had a way to solve these problems, making the Chinese printing system more efficient and practical. If he carved small blocks for each letter of the alphabet, he realized, instead of one large block for a whole page of text, he could reuse the letters over and over again, putting them together with other letters to form lines of type. (This was a solution that worked very well with the Roman alphabet's twenty-six letters, it should be pointed out, but would have been next to impossible for the Chinese to implement with their thousands of pictographs, which is likely why they didn't come up with the idea themselves.) Gutenberg also thought of making the letters out of metal, so they would last longer than wood and could be used many more times. And because the letters were individual units, they could be popped out and replaced with ease. So if a person preparing a document for printing (called a compositor) accidentally used an E instead of an A, he didn't have to scrap the whole block of type and start over, as the Chinese had to do, but could simply take out that E and replace it with an A. Problem solved.

Gutenberg's invention, called movable type, made it easier to spread information to anyone who wanted it. It was the beginning of what is sometimes called the democratization of knowledge – that is, making all the learning contained in books available not just to the rich but to anyone who had a bookstore or library nearby. For merchants and tradesmen and other businesspeople, however, copying documents by hand was still the order of the day. Until the late eighteenth century, most businesses and offices employed copy clerks to duplicate account books, correspondence, contracts, and other important documents. It was the 1780s before people began to experiment with ways to automate the copying process on a small scale, for use in individual businesses. Some of the greatest minds of the next hundred years turned their attention to the problem, including James Watt, the inventor of the steam engine, Thomas Jefferson, and Thomas Edison.

How Does Xeroxing Work?

Chester Carlson's theory was that if you charged a metal plate with static electricity and then shone an image, such as a picture or a sheet of type, onto that plate and exposed the whole thing to light, the image would get recorded as a pattern of positive charges. When negatively charged toner (dry powder) was sprinkled on the plate, it would be attracted to the areas that had been positively charged and would stick to them. If paper was then placed on top, and heat used to bake the toner into the paper, the image would be reproduced.

Sounds simple enough, but Carlson worked for years before he was able to turn his idea into reality. One day, he printed "10-22-38 Astoria" – for the date and the New York City neighborhood where he did his experiments – onto a sheet of paper. His assistant rubbed a metal plate with a cotton cloth to create the static charge they needed, and they exposed the plate to the paper. After holding the exposed plate under a desk lamp for a few moments, they dusted it with powder, pressed to it another sheet of paper, and heated the whole thing almost to the melting point. When they peeled away the second sheet, what did they find? "10-22-38 Astoria."

Still, no one had succeeded in devising an easy-to-use, in-expensive machine for making multiple accurate copies by the time Chester Carlson began his experiments during the depths of the Depression. When he enjoyed that first success in 1938, he must surely have thought companies would be falling all over themselves to fund his research into perfecting the process he called electrophotography. But no one was interested. Chester Carlson carried on in obscurity, laboring away at night and on the weekends and at any other time he had a free moment. His work almost broke him both physically and financially, and it cost him his marriage. But after eight long, lonely years had passed, a small manufacturer of photographic supplies called Haloid finally came on board. The company took a huge gamble that paid off millions of times over, and poor old Chester Carlson was rewarded with an esti-mated $150 million, most of which he gave away to charities and even needy individuals who simply wrote and asked for his help. In 1961, Haloid changed its name to the Xerox Corporation.

In 1946, the process known as electro-photography was renamed xerogra-phy, from the Greek words xeros *for* "dry" *and* graphos *for "writing."*

Y

Yawning

We all know that when we see someone else yawn, we will probably want to yawn ourselves. But you may be surprised to learn that hearing a yawn or even reading about yawning will provoke the same response. In fact, it's likely that you will yawn at least once while you read this piece.

Given that yawning is such a simple behavior – and something we all do – it's amazing how little we understand it. Scientists can't even agree on what causes us to yawn in the first place, let alone explain its effect on us. The traditional theory is that yawning is the body's answer to a lack of oxygen: if we are in a room where there's too little oxygen or too much carbon dioxide, we are supposed to be more susceptible to yawning. The idea is that a yawn is really nothing more than a great big gulp of air, and that all we are trying to do is get more much-needed oxygen to our brains.

But some studies have proven that people yawn just as often when they are being given extra oxygen. And we know that fetuses can yawn in the womb, where lack of oxygen is not an issue (though boredom, another supposed cause of yawning, may be). This has led some scientists to suggest that a yawn merely signals upcoming changes in the body's biology. So a person may yawn when she's getting ready to turn in at night, an indication that she is growing less alert and preparing for sleep. But that same person may also yawn when she first gets up in the morning, a sign that her body is moving from sleep to wakefulness. One scientist showed that elite athletes often yawn right before they compete – proof, certainly, that yawning has nothing to do with boredom or tiredness.

Blind people will often yawn simply from hearing a recording of others yawning.

If there is a connection between yawning and biology, this may explain why it's common among carnivores (meat-eaters like us, as well as cats and dogs) but rarer among herbivores (plant-eaters like deer and horses). Historically, carnivores have required bursts of energy to help them run down and kill their prey; a yawn may have been just the thing to bring about that sudden switch from lazing by the fire outside the cave to sprinting across the landscape in hot pursuit of dinner.

This suggests one possible reason why yawning seems to be contagious. For early man, the sight of one person yawning may have signaled that a change in activity was imminent; any onlookers would yawn too, in an attempt to quickly move themselves to a state of greater alertness. Could this be why the sight or sound of someone yawning still provokes the same response in us today? Perhaps it's like a genetic memory, something that we inherited from our ancient ancestors and still practice, even though it no longer serves a purpose. Yawning, one expert contends, is proof that we are still citizens of that primitive, untamed world we like to think we left behind so many millennia ago.

Z

Zero

Not only is the number zero shaped like a circle, but it also brings us full circle in this book. Like the alphabet, our A word, zero is one of those things we take so much for granted that we don't really appreciate its significance. And also like the alphabet, zero is such a fundamental part of our lives that most of us can't imagine a time when it didn't exist.

It would surprise a lot of people to know, then, that zero didn't gain wide acceptance in the Western world until around 1000 A.D., and that parts of Europe continued to resist the notion until as late as the 1400s. In fact, the idea of zero provoked a great deal of mistrust and even fear. That's a whole lot of fuss over *nothing*.

Our system of numbers – called Arabic numerals, for reasons we'll return to in a moment – is, like the alphabet, a seemingly simple innovation that is actually remarkably ingenious. With just ten figures – 0, 1, 2, 3, 4, 5, 6, 7, 8, and 9 – we are able to create any number we can conceive of. Things weren't always so straightforward, however.

The Egyptians and the Sumerians, who lived in what is now Iraq, were the first to invent ways of counting, probably in about 3000 B.C. The Egyptians created individual hieroglyphics for the numbers one, ten, one hundred, one thousand, and so on, up to a million. (It made sense to these always sensible people to count in multiples of ten, because the very first counters in all societies were our ten fingers.) If an Egyptian wanted to write the number 238, he would simply mark down two of the symbol for a hundred, three of the symbol for ten, and eight of the symbol for one. Because the value of each individual symbol was always the same, it made no difference whether the hieroglyphics were written from left to right or right to left; no matter their order, eight ones, two hundreds, and three tens would always give a total of 238.

Since the value of the numbers didn't depend on their sequence or position, as it does in our system, the Egyptians had no need for zero. Let's say that instead of the 238 of our previous example, they wanted to create the number 208. Rather than using zero to mean "no tens," as we would do, the Egyptians simply wrote down two hundreds and eight ones, with no ten symbols at all.

The main problem with the quite clever Egyptian system – and with the very similar Sumerian one, which went up in multiples of sixty instead of ten – was that large quantities required a whole long series of symbols. To write the number 7,267, for example, an Egyptian needed a mind-boggling twenty-two symbols! This was both awkward and, often, hard to decipher. The solution was to create what is called a place value system, where the position of a symbol in relation to any other symbols determines its value. This is the kind of system we use today. When we look at the number 684, we realize that this stands for six hundreds, eight tens, and four ones. But if we take the same three figures and put them in a different order – 864, let's say – we end up with a totally different number. The place each figure is in tells us its value.

The Babylonians, who were descended from the Sumerians, were the first to introduce a place value system, in about 2000 B.C. Initially, this made things much easier, because they could use the same symbols to represent vastly different numbers, so fewer symbols were needed overall. But the Babylonians quickly encountered a problem: when there was no entry in one of the positions, they had no way of indicating that. Let's say that you wanted to write the number 407 but had no zero to work with. How would you do it? The Babylonians thought of using spaces to indicate the empty spot – in other words, 407 would be written, in our numbers, as 4 [space] 7. Not a bad idea, but sloppy scribes and hurried merchants soon pointed out the obvious flaw: if you weren't careful about spacing, 4 [space] 7 could easily be mistaken for 47. Or even 4007. The Babylonians struggled along with this system for quite a few centuries, but they knew something better was needed.

In around 300 B.C., someone finally came up with the idea of creating a new symbol to fill in that empty space, something like two wedges, or upside-down triangles on sticks, turned on their side. Now it was easy to tell which position a figure was meant to occupy. But this new symbol was strictly a placeholder; unlike our zero, it had no value of its own.

So how did we get from two wedges with no value to the smart little oval with a value of zero? To answer that question, we need to travel thousands of miles east and several centuries forward in time, to the India of the mid-400s A.D. Like the Babylonians, the Indians used a place value system, and like us, they had distinct symbols for one through nine. (Actually, their symbols for one, two, three, and six look remarkably like our own.) They also used a dot to occupy the blank spaces the Babylonians had filled with wedges.

What made their system a cut above anything that had come before was that the Indians understood that that dot, the zero mark, could be so much more than a placeholder. First, they began adding it to the end of a string of numbers to increase them tenfold, just as we do. That little dot tacked onto the end of the number 27 suddenly gave them 270. Next, they gave zero its own value, so that they had a way of representing what's left when a number is subtracted from itself.

Seems so simple that it's hard to imagine it took so many hundreds of years to get to that point. But once there, people

Round and Round We Go

We can't be sure where the idea of using an O as the symbol for zero came from. Many people believe it has something to do with the Greek *omicron*, their letter O and the start of their word for "nothing." Others insist it was just a natural evolution from the Indian dot to a small circle to the larger oval we use today. We do think that the dot the Indians chose to use recalls the counting boards that were common everywhere before written counting systems were developed. People would move stones or seeds from one column to the next, as they do beads on an abacus. These small, round pebbles were probably the inspiration for the little dot. In Latin, the word for a pebble is *calculus*, which gives us both the name of a branch of mathematics and the word "calculate."

must have been falling all over themselves to adopt the Indian numbering system, including their zero, right? Well, not exactly. In fact, many people outside of India were suspicious of zero, and even a little afraid of it.

The problem for Westerners was that zero represented nothing, and nothing was something to fear. They believed that nothing – emptiness, a vacuum, chaos – was all there had been before the world was created, and that nothingness was therefore related to godlessness and best avoided. Indians had an entirely different religious tradition, so they were much more willing to accept the idea that nothing could actually be something.

The Arabs turned the Indian word for zero, sunya, *into* sifr, *meaning "empty." Through the centuries, this became both our modern English "zero" and the word "cipher," used to refer to coded messages.*

In the end, it was the Arabs who brought zero – and the entire Indian counting system – to the West, and that is why we still call our Indian-inspired figures *Arabic* numerals. The Arabs were a bridge between the people of the East and those of the West, for they traveled and traded extensively with both. When Gerbert of Aurillac, a French mathematician and religious scholar living in Spain, saw how Arab traders performed their calculations, he recognized the ingenuity of what was in fact the Indian system. He was determined to spread it throughout the Western world, and he was soon in a unique position to do so – having become Pope Sylvester II in 999.

It still took time for the "new" system to catch on. By the 1200s, most European merchants were using Arabic numerals for their day-to-day business, but ordinary citizens were still resistant. Part of the problem was that Arabic numerals – especially zero – seemed to lend themselves to easy fraud. These were the days before printing was invented, remember, and people wrote all their financial records, and everything else, by hand. If you penned the words "one hundred and seventy-four," it was very difficult for anyone to turn that into anything else. But the figure 174? Add a zero and that becomes 1,740! And zero itself could be turned into a six or a nine with hardly any effort at all.

The invention of the printing press in the mid-1400s removed the last obstacle to zero, and we have been living in harmony with it ever since. In fact, the spread of Arabic numerals in general, once started, proved impossible to stop. In its struggle for acceptance, the Indian counting system launched battles over religion, mathematics, philosophy, and history, but today it is the standard in pretty much every country of the world – even those that do not use the Roman alphabet. Brilliant in its simplicity, it is like a universal language in a world of more than six thousand tongues.

Bibliography

The Alphabet

Johanna Drucker, *The Alphabetic Labyrinth: The Letters in History and Imagination* (London: Thames and Hudson, 1995).

Robert K. Logan, *The Alphabet Effect: The Impact of the Phonetic Alphabet on the Development of Western Civilization* (New York: William Morrow, 1986).

John Man, *Alpha Beta: How Our Alphabet Shaped the Western World* (London: Headline, 2000).

David Sacks, *Language Visible: Unraveling the Mystery of the Alphabet from A to Z* (Toronto: Knopf, 2003).

World Book Encyclopedia articles on the alphabet itself and all the individual letters.

Black

Victoria Finlay, *Travels through the Paintbox* (London: Hodder and Stoughton, 2002).

Margaret Visser, *The Way We Are* (Toronto: HarperPerennial, 1995).

Calendars

Anthony Aveni, *Empires of Time: Calendars, Clocks, and Cultures* (New York: Basic Books, 1989).

David Ewing Duncan, *Calendar: Humanity's Epic Struggle to Determine a True and Accurate Year* (New York: Avon Books, 1998).

Duncan Steel, *Marking Time: The Epic Quest to Invent the Perfect Calendar* (Toronto: John Wiley and Sons, 2000).

Diamonds

Matthew Hart, *Diamond: A Journey to the Heart of an Obsession* (Toronto: Penguin, 2001).

Susanne Steinem Patch, *Blue Mystery: The Story of the Hope Diamond* (New York: Harry Abrams, 1999).

Public Broadcasting System, "Treasures of the World: The Notorious Hope Diamond," www.pbs.org/treasuresoftheworld/a_nav/hope_nav/main_hopfrm.html.

Peter Tyson, "Diamonds in the Sky," www.pbs.org/wgbh/nova/diamond/sky.html.

Easter

Anthony Aveni, *The Book of the Year: A Brief History of Our Seasonal Holidays* (New York: Oxford University Press, 2003).

Venetia Newell, *An Egg at Easter: A Folklore Study* (London: Routledge and Kegan Paul, 1971).

Margaret Visser, *The Way We Are* (Toronto: HarperPerennial, 1995).

Forks

Norbert Elias, *The Civilizing Process*, rev. ed. (London: Blackwell, 1994).

Giovanni Rebora, *Culture of the Fork: A Brief History of Food in Europe*, trans. Albert Sonnenfeld (New York: Columbia University Press, 2001).

Margaret Visser, *The Rituals of Dinner: The Origins, Evolution, Eccentricities and Meaning of Table Manners* (Toronto: HarperPerennial, 2000).

Games

Jack Botermans, Tony Burrett, Pieter van Delft, and Carla van Splunteren, *The World of Games: Their Origins and History* (New York: Facts on File, 1989).

Marcel Danesi, *The Puzzle Instinct: The Meaning of Puzzles in Human Life* (Bloomington: Indiana University Press, 2002).

Alannah Hegedus and Kaitlin Rainey, *Shooting Hoops and Skating Loops: Great Inventions in Sports* (Toronto: Tundra Books, 1999).

Gerda Reith, *The Age of Chance: Gambling and Western Culture* (London: Routledge, 2002).

Gerda Reith, ed., *Gambling: Who Wins? Who Loses?* (Amherst, NY: Prometheus Books, 2003).

Holidays

Anthony Aveni, *The Book of the Year: A Brief History of Our Seasonal Holidays* (New York: Oxford University Press, 2003).

Margaret Visser, *The Way We Are* (Toronto: HarperPerennial, 1995).

Ice Cream

Julio César Centeno, "Vanilla or Trout?: Mad Inventor Creates Bizarre Ice Cream Menu," *Wall Street Journal*, June 18, 1998.

Margaret Visser, *Much Depends on Dinner* (Toronto: HarperPerennial, 2000).

Lee Wardlaw, *We All Scream for Ice Cream!: The Scoop on America's Favorite Dessert* (New York: HarperTrophy, 2000).

Jack-o'-lanterns

Tom Harris, "How Halloween Works," people.howstuffworks.com/halloween.htm.

History Channel, "The History of Halloween," www.historychannel.com/exhibits/halloween/main.html.

Margaret Visser, *The Way We Are* (Toronto: HarperPerennial, 1995).

Kissing

Adrianne Blue, *On Kissing: Travels in an Intimate Landscape* (New York: Kodansha, 1996).

Nicolas J. Perella, *The Kiss: Sacred and Profane* (Berkeley, CA: University of California Press, 1969).

Lipstick

Meg Cohen Ragas and Karen Kozlowski, *Read My Lips: A Cultural History of Lipstick* (San Francisco: Chronicle Books, 1998).

Jessica Pallingston, *Lipstick: The World's Favorite Cosmetic* (New York: St. Martin's Press, 1999).

Money

James Buchan, *Frozen Desire: The Meaning of Money* (New York: Farrar, Straus and Giroux, 1997).

Joe Cribb, *Eyewitness Books: Money* (Toronto: Stoddart, 1990).

Public Broadcasting System, "Secrets of Making Money," www.pbs.org/wgbh/nova/transcripts/2314secr.html.

Numbers

Raymond Lamont Brown, *A Book of Superstitions* (Devon, UK: David and Charles Publishers, 1970).

Iona Opie and Maria Tatem, eds., *A Dictionary of Superstitions* (Oxford: Oxford University Press, 1989).

David Pickering, *Dictionary of Superstitions* (London: Cassell, 1995).

Annemarie Schimmel, *The Mystery of Numbers* (New York: Oxford University Press, 1993).

Richard Wiseman, "2003 UK Superstition Survey," the-ba.net/the-ba/news/uploads/superstition_report2.pdf (the website of the British Association for the Advancement of Science).

Oaths

Geoffrey Hughes, *Swearing: A Social History of Foul Language, Oaths and Profanity in English* (Oxford: Blackwell, 1991).

Peter Tyson, "The Hippocratic Oath Today," www.pbs.org/wgbh/nova/doctors/oath_today.html.

Geoffrey C. Ward, with Ric Burns and Ken Burns, *The Civil War: An Illustrated History* (New York: Knopf, 1992).

Pretzels

Martin Elkort, *The Secret Life of Food: A Feast of Food and Drink History, Folklore, and Fact* (Los Angeles: Jeremy P. Tarcher, 1991).

Eleanor Sullo, "Pretzel History: Some Little Known Facts," oh.essortment.com/pretzelhistory_raxn.htm.

Queen's English

Bill Bryson, *The Mother Tongue: English and How It Got That Way* (New York: HarperPerennial, 2001).

Robert McCrum, William Cran, and Robert MacNeil, *The Story of English* (New York: Penguin, 1987).

Rice

Sri Owen, *The Rice Book* (New York: St. Martin's Press, 1993).

Christian Teubner, *The Rice Bible* (New York: Viking, 1999).

Margaret Visser, *Much Depends on Dinner* (Toronto: HarperPerennial, 2000).

Sideburns

Cyril Leslie Beeching, *A Dictionary of Eponyms* (Oxford: Oxford University Press, 1988).

Allan Peterkin, *One Thousand Beards: A Cultural History of Facial Hair* (Vancouver: Arsenal Pulp, 2001).

Geoffrey C. Ward, with Ric Burns and Ken Burns, *The Civil War: An Illustrated History* (New York: Knopf, 1992).

Tulips

Mike Dash, *Tulipomania: The Story of the World's Most Coveted Flower and the Extraordinary Passions It Aroused* (New York: Three Rivers Press, 2001).

Charles Mackay, *Extraordinary Popular Delusions and the Madness of Crowds* (New York: Three Rivers Press, 1995). First published 1852.

Anna Pavord, *The Tulip* (London: Bloomsbury, 2000).

Underwear

Elaine Benson and John L. Esten, *Unmentionables: A Brief History of Underwear* (New York: Simon and Schuster, 1996).

Lynn Schnurnberger, *Let There Be Clothes* (New York: Workman Publishing, 1991).

Valerie Steele, *The Corset: A Cultural History* (New Haven, CN: Yale University Press, 2001).

Valentines

History Channel, "The History of Valentine's Day," www.historychannel.com/exhibits/valentine/history.html.

Ruth Webb Lee, *A History of Valentines* (New York: Studio Publications, 1952).

Frank Staff, *The Valentine and Its Origins* (London: Lutterworth Press, 1969).

White

Victoria Finlay, *Travels through the Paintbox* (London: Hodder and Stoughton, 2002).

Xeroxing

James Burke, *Connections* (London: Macmillan, 1978).

Ira Flatow, *They All Laughed: The Fascinating Stories behind the Great Inventions That Have Changed Our Lives* (New York: HarperPerennial, 1993).

Yawning

Jay Ingram, "Don't Be Afraid to Yawn While You Read This," *Toronto Star*, Nov. 16, 2003.

Rebecca Raphael, "Is Yawning Contagious?" www.abcnews.go.com/onair/2020/2020_000712_contagiousbehavior_feature.html.

Zero

John D. Barrow, *The Book of Nothing* (London: Jonathan Cape, 2000).

Robert Kaplan, *The Nothing That Is: A Natural History of Zero* (New York: Oxford University Press, 2000).

Charles Seife, *Zero: The Biography of a Dangerous Idea* (New York: Penguin, 2000).

Index